A SHORT HISTORY
OF CHRISTIANITY

A SHORT HISTORY
OF CHRISTIANITY

Written in Collaboration by

ARCHIBALD G. BAKER · EDITOR

MASSEY H. SHEPHERD, JR.

JOHN T. McNEILL

MATTHEW SPINKA

WINFRED E. GARRISON

WILLIAM W. SWEET

Phoenix Books

THE UNIVERSITY OF CHICAGO PRESS

Chicago & London

THE UNIVERSITY OF CHICAGO PRESS, CHICAGO 60637
The University of Chicago Press, Ltd., London

81 80 79 78 77 76   18 17 16 15 14

ISBN: 0-226-03529-8 [clothbound]; 0-226-03530-1 [paperbound]
Library of Congress Catalog Card Number: 40-34185

INTRODUCTION

These are days in which the minds of Christian people are turning more and more to the church as the hope of the world. If this confidence is to be intelligent, it must be based upon a knowledge of what the church has accomplished through the centuries and what it has failed to accomplish.

With this history the rank and file of church members are none too familiar. They know something of New Testament times, something of present-day church activities, possibly something of Luther, Calvin, or John Knox. They talk familiarly of the Church Universal, of the Body of Christ, and of similar mystical concepts. But of the church as a historical religious movement, wrestling with the issues of each succeeding century, struggling with the state and the world, giving shape to its doctrinal orthodoxy and institutional form as best it can, time and again breaking out spontaneously beyond the bounds of ecclesiastical conformity, now hibernating through a long winter of worldly coldness and then awakening afresh in a great spiritual revival, it may be of St. Francis, of Wesley, of Moody—of this *continuing church* few Christians have any adequate idea.

This can be easily accounted for. Most church histories are too long for the ordinary reader. The majority of Protestants have looked upon one thousand years of this history as the "great apostasy" which must be repudiated. People find little of interest in doctrinal disputes, political intrigues, and the almost endless mass of dates and details which on the surface seem to have little connection with the vital issues of our modern world. But suddenly this story of Christianity has assumed an importance which can no longer be neglected.

To meet this new interest and in response to the accelerated tempo of the age, the authors have prepared a digest of church history. The book is planned for the use of the serious reader who has only a limited time at his disposal. It is also designed as a textbook for study classes. The material has been cast into the structural form of thirty-two sections, which may be arranged in a series of lessons according to the convenience of the study group.

While there has been consultation between the various authors in order to give structural unity to the story of the church, each writer is responsible only for his own contribution.

The understanding of history calls for factual knowledge and intelligent interpretation. For fuller equipment diligent students will find it advisable to consult at least some of the books listed in the Bibliography.

THE EDITOR

TABLE OF CONTENTS

CHAPTER   PAGE

I. THE RISE OF CHRISTIANITY 1

Massey H. Shepherd, Jr., Instructor in Divinity, Episcopal Theological School, Cambridge, Massachusetts

II. CHRISTIANITY AND THE FALL OF ROME 33

Massey H. Shepherd, Jr.

III. CHRISTIANITY IN MEDIEVAL EUROPE 66

John T. McNeill, Professor of the History of European Christianity, Divinity School, University of Chicago

IV. CHRISTIANITY IN THE REFORMATION ERA . . . 99

John T. McNeill

V. THE HISTORY OF EASTERN ORTHODOXY 135

Matthew Spinka, Associate Professor of Church History, Divinity School, University of Chicago

VI. CHRISTIANITY IN MODERN EUROPE 168

Winfred E. Garrison, Associate Professor of Church History, Divinity School, University of Chicago

VII. CHRISTIANITY IN THE AMERICAS 199

William W. Sweet, Professor of the History of American Christianity, Divinity School, University of Chicago

VIII. CHRISTIANITY ENCIRCLES THE GLOBE 236

Archibald G. Baker, Associate Professor of Missions, Divinity School, University of Chicago

BIBLIOGRAPHY 265

INDEX 267

CHAPTER I

THE RISE OF CHRISTIANITY

1. Christian Origins

The Roman Empire.—Jesus Christ was born "when the fulness of time was come." This confident assertion made by the apostle Paul is amply confirmed by history. Like a fertile field to the newly planted seed, the environment in which the Christian movement had its beginnings was extraordinarily favorable to its development and spread. Less than a generation before the birth of Jesus the Roman Empire was established by Caesar Augustus. Thus was brought to completion a process of political unification, begun by the conquests of Alexander the Great, of the lands and ancient cultures already bound together geographically by the Mediterranean Sea. On the north the Empire was bounded by the Rhine and the Danube, on the east by the fertile Tigris-Euphrates Valley, on the south by the great African desert, and on the west by the Atlantic Ocean.

Rome governed this vast and varied dominion as a military despotism; yet its power was exercised chiefly in the maintenance of public peace and the collection of taxes and tribute. Administration of justice was remarkably fair and efficient. Business and trade flourished as tariff barriers were eliminated and easy lines of communication made possible by the govern-

1

ment's extensive road construction (chiefly for military purposes) and riddance of piracy on the water routes. Common use of the Greek language fostered the intercourse of people, ideas, and commercial traffic. Toward business enterprises and cultural pursuits Rome maintained a strict policy of laissez faire. Cities of cosmopolitan population grew to unprecedented size, magnificently adorned with artistic monuments and buildings and endowed with excellent schools of rhetoric and philosophy. Large numbers of people, however, remained poor and depressed, caught in the maelstrom of unrestricted competition and dependent upon the largess of the emperor or wealthy patrons for their very food, as well as amusement. Programs of social betterment organized on any scale comparable to the public need were virtually nonexistent.

Few periods of human history have exhibited more varied and widespread religious interests. Both the imperial and the local governments supported as public services official cults of the time-honored gods of storied myth for their sanction and benefaction to the commonweal. After the death of Augustus the custom of ruler worship, long known to the peoples of the eastern provinces, was increasingly applied to the Roman emperors both living and dead. In the case of wise and beneficent rulers such devotion was as genuinely religious as it was patriotic and prudent.

Educated and cultured people found personal religious satisfaction in the study and practice of philosophy, which concerned itself not only with deep speculations about the causes, nature, and meanings of things but also with the problems and duties of every-day living. A religion of this sort was highly individualistic, for the philosophers were not organized, for the most part, in associations of clearly defined membership. Though there was no lack of definite systems of philosophy, such as the Stoic, Epicurean, or Platonic, most devotees preferred to be eclectic and choose from the various schools of thought such ideals and practices as appealed to them.

For great numbers of people the most satisfying religious experiences were to be found in the cults known as mystery religions. These were secret societies, mostly of oriental origin, whose "mysteries" were imparted only to those who underwent a dramatic and emotionally exciting rite of initiation. By virtue of this rite an initiate was "reborn" and obtained an earnest of an eternal life of bliss after death. The guarantor of immortality was none other than the god of the cult himself, who in ages long past had suffered a violent death but had been restored to life. Since the mystery religions were open to all persons regardless of race or class, many folk dispirited by their ill lot in this world found in them a source of hope and comfort. Active propaganda and extensive interchange of ideas gave to the mystery religions a preponderant influence upon the religious climate of the Roman Empire.

Judaism.—In all important centers of population in the Empire Jewish people were to be found in great numbers. In Alexandria, Egypt, for example, they occupied a sizable quarter of the city and enjoyed communal self-government. Though their religious and social exclusiveness won them the scornful contempt of the masses, many thoughtful persons were attracted by the nobility of their worship of one God and their ethical standards. To such inquirers the Jews were not slow to improve their relations and to recommend their religious principles in terms approximating the best philosophical thought of the times. The writings of several of their apologists have come down to us, notably the works of Philo of Alexandria, a contemporary of Jesus, and one of the most respected thinkers of his day.

Worship and instruction in the synagogues were open to all comers and were carried on, outside of Palestine, in the Greek language. Indeed before the Christian Era the Old Testament had been translated into Greek—a version of the Scriptures known as the Septuagint. Early Christian missionaries found in the synagogues of the Jewish dispersion a fertile field to begin their work of evangelization, not only among the Jews but also among numbers of gentile "God-fearers."

In Palestine Jewish hostility to all things gentile was far more sharp. Remembrance of the glories of David and Solomon's kingdom, combined with the fresh experience of complete independence for about one hundred years before the coming of the Romans under Pompey in 63 B.C., made the Palestinian Jews exceedingly restive. Periodic outbreaks of revolt forced upon them a heavier hand of Roman military power than was the case in many other provinces of the Empire.

Those who realized the futility of armed resistance took comfort in the lively hopes, entertained in almost all circles with varying degrees of vividness, that God himself would shortly intervene to smite the foreign oppressor and establish a new age in which his people would enjoy the full fruition of his promises made to them of old by the prophets. Imagination was often pressed to extravagant limits to describe the incidents attendant upon the imminent day of judgment when God or his "Anointed One," the Messiah, would intervene to order a new heaven and a new earth.

The center of Jewish religious life was the temple in Jerusalem, with its daily round of sacrificial offerings of praise, penitence, and supplication. On great festival occasions, such as Passover or Pentecost, pilgrims assembled here from all parts of the Empire. At the head of the priestly caste, who performed the temple rites, was a small party of wealthy, aristocratic families, known as Sadducees, from whose number the government appointed the high priest, the chief civil and religious officer of the Jewish people. The Sadducees were arch-conservatives, distrustful of all innovations in religious belief and practice, but not unwilling to accommodate themselves to many gentile habits of living.

Their more successful rivals for popular religious leadership were the Pharisees, who dominated the teaching and worship of the synagogues. They were zealous advocates of uncompromising obedience to the law of God as laid down in the Scriptures. But in their effort to make this law apply to every possible circumstance and situation which might arise in daily life, they developed a cumbrous load of traditions, known only to the learned, and more burdensome than the mass of folk were able or willing to bear. Thus formalism and pride were their besetting sins. Yet it is only fair to say that their emphasis upon repentance for sin and the necessity of righteousness in all endeavors served as a real leaven for good in Jewish religion.

Jesus.—In a devout home of humble though sturdy village folk Jesus was born and reared. His call to his life's work was evoked by the preaching of one John, an ascetic prophet living near the Jordan River, who had attracted great crowds by his forewarning of the imminent coming of God's new age and the need of repentance to prepare for it. With many others Jesus accepted baptism from John's hands. Returning to his native district of Galilee, he at once began to preach as opportunity afforded, both in the synagogues and out, the "good news" of God's promised redemption.

The utter sincerity and strength of Jesus' character and the commanding conviction of his message won an enthusiastic reception; and we are told that "the common people heard him gladly." Wonders of healing which he performed attracted the needy, the curious, and the skeptical. To Jesus they were evident signs that God was already at work in the world to bring faithful men under his rule. He became conscious during his short-lived ministry that he himself was God's chosen Messiah to usher in the new day of righteousness—a view shared by his intimate disciples who knew him best, so much so that one was ready to take up arms to bring in the kingdom by violence. Nothing could have been more alien to the spirit of Jesus' teaching. Entrance into the Kingdom of Heaven could be given only to those who with hearty repentance, full faith, and unbounded charity to their fellow-men yielded their lives in perfect submission to the will of God.

Opposition to Jesus on the part of the religious leaders quickly crystallized. They rejected his claim to messiahship—for was he not simply the carpenter's son from Nazareth? Jesus' sensitive insight into the inner spirit of true religion had pricked the shell of formalism with which they incrusted their piety and had exposed their hypocrisy and spiritual obtuseness. Seeing the increasing influence which he exercised among the people brought sharply to focus on the occasion of his pilgrimage to Jerusalem to celebrate the Passover festival, they accused him to the Roman governor, Pontius Pilate, as a fomenter of sedition. His end was thereby sealed. The Roman government had been troubled by so many "messianic" disturbances in Palestine that justice to Jesus yielded to fear of public disorder. Jesus was crucified between two thieves.

Christian beginnings.—The intimate disciples of Jesus, fearful of their own lives and disillusioned by their master's ignominious death, hastened home to Galilee. But Jesus appeared to them alive again! In joyous assurance of his resurrection and exaltation at God's right hand in heaven to appear again in glory to establish the longed-for kingdom, the disciples hurried back to Jerusalem. At the festival of Pentecost an extraordinary outburst of the prophetic spirit encouraged them to preach boldly the marvelous news about Jesus and to call men to repentance and baptism in his name. Their enthusiasm was contagious. Many accepted baptism and joined the new fellowship where God's Spirit appeared so active and real. Daily propaganda was conducted from Solomon's portico in the temple with surprising success. Efforts of the religious authorities to silence the leaders of the new movement were futile. Indeed, some influential Pharisees were little inclined to repressive measures, if not openly favorable toward the movement.

The believers in Jesus remained loyal to all the customs of Jewish worship and ways of living. In fact, they considered themselves to be "the true Israel" and inheritors of all of God's promises to the chosen people. They assembled frequently in their homes for prayer and mutual edification and continued the practice, observed by Jesus and his intimate disciples, of common meals. In the "breaking of bread" they seemed vividly aware of the living presence of Jesus with them and sensed some joyful foretaste of banqueting with him in the age to come. Most of them were exceedingly poor, and distribution of goods to their several needs was provided out of a common chest, to which many contributed all that they possessed.

Many Greek-speaking Jews of the dispersion, who had returned to Jerusalem to live, were attracted to the movement. When some of their widows complained of being slighted in the daily dispensing of food, seven men were appointed to look after their needs. The leader of this group, Stephen, proved himself a no less able preacher. Some of his views, notably those about the temple and its services, were alarmingly unorthodox. He was arraigned before the religious authorities and condemned to be stoned. A vigorous persecution of his sympathizers followed, led by Saul of Tarsus, a relentless Pharisee. The result of this conflict was to scatter many of the believers outside the confines of Jerusalem and thus unexpectedly to start the Christian movement upon its world-wide mission.

2. Formation of the Church

The gentile mission.—Those who left Jerusalem to escape the fate of Stephen carried the story of Jesus to all who would give them audience. Soon the community of believers in Jerusalem was apprised of similar bands of disciples in Samaria, Joppa, Caesarea, Damascus, and even in distant Antioch. More incredible still was the news that Saul the persecutor (later known as Paul) had experienced a vision of the risen Jesus and had received baptism in Damascus, where he had gone with the intent of molesting the believers.

The home community in Jerusalem endeavored to maintain a general oversight of the new "churches." Visits were paid them by Peter and John, and other less eminent leaders, to see that the new communities were in full possession of God's Spirit, and to encourage them in prayers and exhortation. Contributions to the poor fund of the Jerusalem church, collected from time to time, helped to maintain a bond of sympathy with the mother-community. At the head of the church in Jerusalem was James, a brother of Jesus, who was highly respected by the Jews for his piety and sanctity. With him were associated a council of elders, including the twelve companions of Jesus (such as Peter and John) known as "apostles." The decisions and counsels of these men carried great weight in all the churches.

At Antioch, where the disciples were first called Christians, the good news about Jesus was presented not only to Jews but also to Gentiles. Thus a new field of work was opened which proved so promising that the Antioch Christians felt moved by the Spirit to send out two missionaries to extend the area of Christian propaganda. Barnabas and Paul were selected for the task. Their first journey took them to the island of Cyprus and the cities of the provinces on the southern coast of Asia Minor. The results of this mission showed that Gentiles were as willing, if not more so, as Jews, to accept the Christian message. Missionary ventures were accordingly launched on a wider scale and within a generation had established Christian churches in cities all over the Empire as far as Rome.

The nucleus of membership of the new societies was gathered from the synagogues, where both Jews and Gentiles would already be familiar with the promise of God's Messiah and kingdom. Naturally most of the Jews were unconvinced that Jesus of Nazareth was the Christ (i.e., the Messiah). Accordingly, Christian believers were invariably expelled from the synagogues and forced to organize as independent churches. Of Paul's extensive missionary activities we are fortunate in having a fairly full record in his extant letters and in the Book of Acts, much of which is by an eyewitness. However, it must not be forgotten that Paul was only one of many devoted pioneers in Christian evangelization.

Barnabas and Paul never required their gentile converts to assume any obligation of fulfilling the minutiae of religious customs and practices of the Jewish law as laid down in the Old Testament. The gracious Spirit of the risen Christ was a possession of all believers equally, a fact which proved that the regulations of the old law were unnecessary, if not an obstacle, to the admission of all mankind into the inheritance of God's kingdom. For a strict Jew, however, any such principle made common life with Gentiles within the church impossible, particularly the custom of eating together the fellowship meal. Leaders of the church in Jerusalem looked somewhat askance at the freedom of social intercourse enjoyed in Paul's churches; and not a few Jewish emissaries visited the new churches with an insistence that gentile converts to Christianity become thoroughgoing Jews as well.

The upshot of the question was a bitter controversy, which ended in a compromise arrived at in a council of Christian leaders in Jerusalem. Paul and Barnabas won for their gentile Christians a complete freedom from the ceremonial requirements of the Jewish law but promised to maintain the standards of moral conduct for which the Jews were conspicuous and to make no peace with the idolatrous practices of gentile religion. A further promise to continue the contributions to poor relief in Jerusalem considerably helped to ease wounded feelings! The decisions of this council were of far-reaching consequence for the future of Christianity. They marked the end of any predominant Jewish influence upon its growth and development. Most Jews were implacably hostile to any compromising with their cherished religious traditions. The Jewish Christians of Palestine, led by the family of Jesus, maintained a precarious existence for several generations and then disappeared into historical oblivion.

Problems of a new generation.—The death of the original leaders who had known Jesus in the flesh or who had enjoyed intimate association with his companions created a host of problems for the surviving and growing churches. How were the norms of religious belief and moral behavior to be preserved in the preaching and teaching of the communities? What persons were to exercise authoritative judgments in such matters? How were the churches to keep in close touch with one another to consolidate their efforts and prevent disruptive tendencies caused by innovators from within and opponents from without? In view of the evident delay of God's intervention in the world to establish his kingdom of righteousness, what attitudes should Christians adopt toward the society in which they made their livelihood—one of withdrawal and animosity or one of leavening and redeeming it into a Christian kingdom on this earth?

One of the first accomplishments of the "second"

generation of Christianity was the preservation in written record of the life and teachings of Jesus. Stories and sayings of the master, gathered from first- or secondhand witnesses, were circulated orally by missionaries and teachers. These varied in detail according to the particular need for their guidance in points of belief or behavior. Collections of related stories and sayings were then made and probably written down. The oldest "gospel" we now have is that attributed to Mark, written shortly after A.D. 70. About twenty years later were written the gospels of Matthew and Luke, which used much of Mark's materials plus a great quantity of parables and sayings. These were but a few of many attempts to recount the "good news" of Jesus. Only four gospels, however, succeeded in winning the approval of all the churches as reliable and authoritative records. To these gospels were shortly added a collection of letters of Paul and several other documents of merited importance which claimed authorship by original leaders of the movement. Thus a "New Testament" was gradually formed as a companion authority with the old Jewish Scriptures for the guidance of the churches' life.

The Gnostics.—The Old Testament was not kept by the churches without a struggle. As numbers of converts to Christianity increased from the gentile world, many were found ready to interpret the message of Jesus without reference to its Jewish roots. Jesus appealed to them in the same way as the gods of the mystery religions—as a dying and rising Savior who guaranteed a blessed life after death to those initiated into his religion by baptism. Despairing of happiness and justice in this world, they set their hopes on the future. Indeed some regarded the entire material universe as the work of an evil creator-god. Jesus had come as a divine redeemer from an unknown god of goodness to reveal to men a secret "knowledge" and way of escape from the meshes of evil, material existence in which they were caught. They denied that Jesus himself had really been a man of flesh and blood, or had really suffered and died as a human being, but asserted that he only seemed to be so—a god masquerading as a man. Beliefs such as these had a wide vogue for a time and were advocated by many able and deeply religious teachers. They came to be known as Gnostics (from a Greek word *gnosis*, meaning "knowledge").

Responsible leaders of the churches in many quarters disapproved of the views of the Gnostics as too radical a departure from the traditions of Christian teaching which had been handed down from the first apostles and missionaries of Christianity. A notable defender of "the apostolic tradition" of Christian faith was Irenaeus, a native of Asia Minor, who later became head of the Christian church in Lyons in southern Gaul. About the year 185 appeared his monumental *Refutation of False Knowledge*, which effectively exposed the danger of Gnostic teaching to the historic foundations of the Christian gospel.

During the second century Gnostic teachers and their followers were gradually expelled from fellowship in the Christian communities. Some of them formed rival "churches" of their own. To safeguard themselves from further conflict of this sort, most of the churches drew up short confessions of faith to be accepted by all persons admitted to baptism. These "creeds" asserted that the God and Father of the Lord Jesus Christ was the same God who created the heavens and the earth (i.e., the God of the Old Testament); that Jesus himself, though of divine origin and nature, was nonetheless a true man, who truly suffered, died, and rose again; and that the resurrection to eternal life which he promised his disciples would be of their material bodies as well as of their souls. The creed adopted by the church in Rome survives to the present day—with a few additions—in the so-called Apostles' Creed.

Church government.—From earliest times the churches were edified by a variety of ministers—apostles, prophets, teachers, healers, etc.—who exercised their peculiar gifts according as God's Spirit severally endowed them. General oversight of each church was in the hands of a committee of older men, called presbyters, just as in the Jewish synagogues. From their number were appointed one or more "bishops" (in Greek, *episcopoi*) who, with the assistance of several "deacons," had a special gift of administering and ruling. The bishops presided at the assemblies for worship and were especially charged with receiving and distributing the donations of the members for purposes of common expenses and charity to the poor and needy.

As the churches grew in numbers the bishops' pastoral and financial duties naturally assumed considerable importance. They were thus in a favorable position to deal with the crises which arose when Gnostic and other teachers of novel doctrines came forth to instruct the faithful. With the counsel of the presbyters they decided who should be allowed to address the congregations over which they presided. The result was a concentration of authority in all matters in the hands of the bishops. This tendency was further accentuated by the custom, begun in the churches of Asia Minor and Syria toward the end of the first century, of electing a single "monarchical" bishop in each church. By the middle of the second century most of the churches had adopted the system of one bishop in each church (i.e., in each community). The system of episcopal government thus evolved served both to consolidate the local churches from disruptive forces and to create authoritative intermediaries in every church for the exchange of interests common to all the Christian communities.

Miscellaneous assemblies of Christians without the bishop's permission were no longer allowed. The entire Christian community gathered every Sunday morning before daybreak for worship at a place appointed by the bishop. Utterances of prophets and preachers were approved before being presented to the congregation. The old common meal of the societies was reduced to a symbolic act—partly because unfortunate excesses at the meals had compromised their religious significance and partly because increase in membership made them impossible to manage. After reading and expounding of the Scriptures, bread and wine and other gifts were brought to the altar, and prayers of intercession for the church's needs and for all men generally were offered. Then the bishop in the name of the people offered over the bread and wine a great prayer of thanksgiving for God's wonderful works of creation and redemption. The elements so blessed were then distributed by the deacons to the people, and what remained was carried to the sick and absent. Thus the worship of the church was taking on a more formal and ordered aspect.

3. THE CHURCH SURVIVES PERSECUTION

Opposition to Christianity.—The Roman government was exceedingly tolerant of all religious cults and interfered in their activities only when it considered them to be foils for treasonable plots. It expected that all subjects be loyal to the official state religion, which early came to mean primarily the worship of the emperor. This requirement was not alien to pagan religious ideas, for the Gentiles never looked upon any one deity as necessarily the sole object of worship. A wise exception to the rule was granted the Jews, however. To leave them contemptuously alone in their religious exclusiveness was an expedient policy, less troublesome to the peace than an attempt to force upon them what they despised as idolatry.

As long as Christianity remained simply a sect within Judaism, it was able to enjoy a similar immunity from governmental interference. But when the Jews made it known in no uncertain terms that they would have nothing to do with the new movement, and when the membership of the churches became predominantly Gentile, the situation was radically altered. If called to the test, Christians would have to choose between God or Caesar, or, as in gentile cults, to accept both. They took the former alternative. Jesus the Jew had taught that there is but one God, and him only should one serve.

History has not spared the record of the original occasion of conflict between Christianity and the state or of the precise terms of the law outlawing the movement and punishing by death the profession of the Christian name. The most common charge leveled against the Christians was atheism; for the gentile mind could not conceive of a religious worship without idols and temples. That Christians were enemies of the social order was no less widely believed. The Christian expectation of the imminent end of the world when Christ would come in glory to establish God's kingdom appeared treasonable, to say the least. Moreover, Christians found it impossible to participate in many social and cultural pursuits of the times because of their mixture with idolatrous practices. Economic tension was aggravated whenever Christians increased in considerable numbers in a community; for profitable temple revenues and markets in offerings for pagan sacrifices would drop to alarmingly low levels.

Many scurrilous stories were circulated from mouth to mouth of unspeakable orgies of immorality taking place at Christian meetings, which were held, of necessity, in secret. To the educated and cultured classes Christianity seemed a specially detestable superstition, with its recruits won chiefly from the very dregs of society for the worship of a crucified criminal! The Jewish origin of Christianity made it all the more despicable to most Gentiles. Even the few thoughtful persons who were willing to give the movement any serious consideration dismissed it as a foolish and novel invention without prestige of ancient myth or ritual.

Christian apologists.—During the first few generations of its development the Christian movement was too obscure to attract general notice or systematized repressive measures. Outbreaks against the Christians were local and sporadic and allowed sufficient breathing space for them to grow steadily and quietly. There was, of course, the famous persecution at Rome under the emperor Nero (A.D. 54–68), when numberless Christians, including possibly the great apostles Peter and Paul, were made the scapegoats for the fire that destroyed a large section of the city. Little more of a definite nature is known of Christian martyrdoms until the reign of Trajan (A.D. 98–117), when we hear of persecution in Bithynia, a province of Asia Minor, under the governor Pliny, and also of the fate of Ignatius, bishop of the church in Antioch, and several companions, who were brought to Rome to be cast before wild beasts in the arena for the amusement of the populace. From this time on the records become more abundant of the horrible tortures to which condemned witnesses of the faith were subjected.

By the second century, however, the church had

won to its cause representatives from all classes of society. Those who possessed a fair degree of literary talent began to publish a series of treatises in defense of Christianity. Typical of these apologists was a Greek from Palestine, named Justin, who came to Rome some time after his conversion to Christianity and there set up a school like those of the philosophers. To interested inquirers he gave lectures on Christian faith and morals and expositions of the Scriptures. He was martyred about the year 165. A brilliant advocate of the Christian cause appeared a generation later in North Africa in the person of a lawyer named Tertullian. His *Apology* in Latin displayed a rich store of learning and a gifted and salty style. By the middle of the third century the opposition of the educated classes to Christianity had met its match in a treatise entitled *Against Celsus*, written in refutation of a book against the Christians by a pagan philosopher. Its author, a Christian scholar, Origen, will be discussed in the next section.

The apologists had little trouble in answering the scandalous gossip about the Christian societies and in defending the good citizenship and loyalty of Christians to the government. They stressed constantly the high moral ideals and character of the Christians to prove them the most stable and law-abiding element of the population. They returned the attack on this score by bitter denunciation of the obscenities frequently to be found in gentile religions and the many disgusting stories in the myths of the pagan gods. They quoted the best thinkers and writers of gentile philosophy to show how they had wrestled with the illogical absurdities of worshiping multitudinous deities and how they had approached the conception of one supreme God, who was now finally revealed in the Christian religion.

Taking much of their fire from earlier Jewish apologists, the Christian defenders argued that the revelation of God in the Old Testament was the real source of all the better religious ideas expounded by the philosophers, since Moses had lived much earlier than they. Extensive use was made of the Old Testament prophets to show how Jesus had fulfilled their predictions. This, together with the miracles which Jesus performed, was sufficient evidence that he was the Son of God and the revealer of saving truth. Much emphasis was placed on the resurrection of Jesus as a guaranty of eternal life to his followers. To express the divine character of Jesus, the apologists made much use of the term "Logos," which was widely used by philosophers to denote the rational principle exhibited in the whole order of nature and in the mind of man. The Logos was the reason and wisdom of God manifest in the world. The apologists claimed that Jesus incarnated in a human life to the fullest degree this reason and wisdom of the mind of God.

Systematic persecution.—It was not until the year 250 that the Roman government took systematic steps to stamp out the Christian movement, though repressive measures in localized areas had recurred in all parts of the Empire with distressing frequency and virulence. "Christians to the lions!" was a common demand of bloodthirsty masses who crowded the public shows and games in the amphitheaters. Popular accusation, rather than any resolute search by the magistrates, was the chief agent of conviction.

During the third century the Empire suffered a number of external and internal crises in economic and military affairs which seriously threatened to shatter its unity. In view of this situation, the emperor Decius, a devout and conservative pagan, believed the old gods of the state should be besought by the entire population for their strengthening aid to the tottering state. Accordingly, he issued an edict requiring every person without exception to appear before the magistrates to offer sacrifice to the official deities. In this way he would be able to force the large number of Christians to pay their proper religious dues to the commonweal. The edict was a stunning blow to the churches. Many endured martyrdom; some found escape in hiding; but great numbers of the faithful, surprised with a sudden fear of losing life and property, apostatized or bribed the officials to give them certificates stating that they had sacrificed. Decius died the following year (251), and persecution ceased. The church had survived but was severely shaken. Again in 257 the emperor Valerian instigated a general persecution, aimed this time principally at the bishops and clergy. This lasted until his capture and death at the hands of the Persians in 260.

If the gods were angry with the temporal state, their tury was not abated by the attack on the Christians. Calamities continued to befall the Empire. During the succeeding two decades and a half the Empire came dangerously near to complete dissolution. For the Christians the period was one of unprecedented growth in numbers and influence. Valerian's successor, Gallienus, restored to them their properties and allowed them freedom of assembly. Imposing church buildings were erected for the first time. So openly were church affairs carried on that a synod of bishops in Antioch actually asked an emperor (Aurelian) to help them enforce a decision of deposition of a bishop convicted of heresy.

A final testing, longer and more violent, was yet to come. After the emperor Diocletian had restored order to the chaotic political and economic affairs of the Empire, a general persecution of Christianity was initiated in 303, largely through the instigation of his co-ruler Galerius. Diocletian retired from office shortly afterwards, but Galerius continued a savage repression, principally in the eastern provinces, until he issued on his deathbed in 311 an edict of toleration.

A signal factor in the success of the church in surviving these dreadful ordeals was the wise policy which it adopted after the Decian persecution toward those Christians who had "lapsed," or apostatized. The leader in formulating this policy was Cyprian, the bishop of Carthage, who himself fell a victim under Valerian. Most of those who gave way to force and compromised their faith did so from an understandable human weakness rather than from any real desire to leave the church. It was therefore decided that after a reasonable period of discipline and penitence such backsliders might be readmitted to the communion of the church and given a second chance. Many of the martyrs themselves gave approval to the forgiveness of their weaker brethren. There were also, to be sure, irreconcilable opponents to any proposal of leniency toward the apostates. In Rome a presbyter named Novatian led a group which separated from the church rather than be a party to the readmission of "lapsed" Christians to communion. The tolerant policy of the great church as a whole, however, salvaged many sincere penitents and contributed much to the rebuilding of the decimated ranks of the faithful.

To the valiant athletes who contended unto death the church paid its highest honors. Their names were carefully kept in the records of the church, and their "birthdays" into eternal life remembered by annual celebrations at their tombs. Their baptism by blood represented the utmost glory that a Christian could attain, and in a very real sense their blood was the seed of the church. In their constancy under the most excruciating tortures they won many to a faith worth dying for. To the church the martyrs bequeathed for all time a legacy of uncompromising hostility to any claim of the state upon the Christian conscience to supreme devotion; and their remembrance is a continual reminder that the Christian's citizenship is in heaven.

4. CHRISTIAN LIFE IN GRECO-ROMAN SOCIETY

Attractiveness of Christianity.—A consistent factor in the appeal which Christianity made to the masses of people, despite the virulent opposition recounted in the preceding section, was its unique capacity for meeting the social needs of the age. In the Christian societies, as nowhere else, men and women found a warm and friendly fellowship which gave them both a sense of individual worth and a sure support in days of want and trouble. This was no little satisfaction in times when many were set adrift from old social and economic moorings by the flood tide of ruthless competitive business and mixing of diverse populations set in motion by the creation of an empire of such vast extent.

It is true that there were innumerable clubs and guilds and trade associations which afforded a modicum of social fellowship and mutual aid under the sanction and patronage of sundry pagan deities. These were purely local organizations, whereas Christianity was a world-wide society. The credential of baptism gave a Christian immediate access to a circle of sympathetic friends in any community to which he might move where there was a Christian church. Hospitality to the stranger was a cardinal virtue of Christian teaching and was provided, if need be, by the bishop out of the treasury of the church. The churches also acted as employment agencies for members out of a job and insured means of support to those unable to find work.

Within the church, members enjoyed social equality regardless of their station in worldly affairs. Master and slave, citizen and subject, rich and poor shared a common table and, if personally qualified, were alike eligible for any office in the community. The dignity and worth of the individual man, though he be a slave, had been a common preachment of gentile philosophers. Christianity put the idea into practice. No attempt was made by the churches, however, to deal with problems of social inequality, such as slavery, in society generally. Even if they had had such a vision, it would have been impossible to promote any constructive program of social betterment in view of their unfavorable political situation. If a Christian slave served a heathen master, he was taught to be honest and obedient and to endeavor to win his master to the faith by the evident nobility of his own character. But under no circumstance was a Christian slave to perform any duty which compromised his religion even though he might suffer death for his disobedience. Church funds were frequently allocated to deserving slaves to assist them in buying their freedom from oppressive pagan masters.

Certain occupations were not allowed anyone wishing to be a Christian in good standing—principally those connected of necessity with pagan religious practices or social vice. Magistrates and public officials were banned, because their duties required participation in rites and ceremonies of the state cults. Sculptors and painters were debarred because their principal trade was in idols and pictures of the heathen gods. Likewise actors and performers in the public games carried the taint of idolatry and immorality. Exceptions were made in the case of schoolteachers if they were unable to find other employment. Much of the literature which they used in teaching was full of stories about the gods, often of a very licentious nature. Opinion was divided as to whether a Christian could be a soldier. The difficulty was not so much due to objection to the occupation as such as to the fact that military discipline frequently forced the soldier to take oaths or associate in ceremonies which were definitely idolatrous. There were, however, many Christians in the army, who served as missionaries of Christian faith on the farthest frontiers of the Empire.

Christian family life.—There was no more marked difference between Christianity and its environing world than in their respective ideals of family life. Divorce was particularly rife in gentile society, and infanticide and abortion were by no means uncommon. The church insisted upon the indissoluble character of the marriage tie; and many looked with disfavor upon a second marriage after the death of a husband or wife. Indeed, so great was the Christian reaction to the loose sexual ethics of pagans that celibacy was highly esteemed and among some Christians regarded as more honorable in the sight of God than marriage. The nurture and training of children in Christian standards of conduct was a prime duty. How early the custom of infant baptism arose it is impossible to say; but it was undoubtedly observed as early as the second century. Some Christians opposed the practice on the grounds that in later life a person baptized in infancy might fall into grievous sin and hence lose his hope of eternal salvation.

Mixed marriages between pagans and Christians

were discouraged but not forbidden. They frequently led to broken homes because of conflict arising out of different standards of social behavior. A constant problem faced by the churches was the preponderance of women members over men, particularly of women from the upper classes. Unless these women adopted a celibate life, as many of them did, most of them would have to find mates outside the Christian fellowship. The laws of the state forbade their marriage to slaves. However, Bishop Callistus of Rome (d. 223) was willing to recognize such unions as valid in the eyes of the church, despite the law and conservative opponents within the church, provided the parties concerned remained faithful to each other. Especial care was given by the churches to all widows and orphans among them. Widows of advanced age were formed into a distinct "order" and given specific duties of charitable service under the direction of the bishop. Decent burial was provided for the poor out of church funds; while wealthy members allowed the use of family property for Christian cemeteries.

Economic growth.—Extremes of wealth and poverty were widely characteristic of society in the Empire and tended to increase as time went on. In the earliest days of the Christian movement membership of the church was recruited almost entirely from the very poor classes. Reflecting this condition, the church took a hostile attitude toward wealth and considered riches a well-nigh insurmountable stumbling-block to entrance into the Kingdom of Heaven. The gradual infiltration of well-to-do people into the church's fellowship and their serviceable charities to the needs of fellow-Christians brought considerable modification in the church's outlook. By the end of the second century a Christian teacher in Alexandria, Clement, could answer his query in a sermon entitled "Who Is the Rich Man That Is Saved?" with a positive affirmation of the good and useful purposes which a wealthy Christian might serve.

Regular contributions, once a week or once a month were paid by all Christians into the church treasury according to their means. These funds were devoted almost entirely to charity, for there were little or no "running expenses" of the churches. Officers served without remuneration, and places of assembly were afforded in the homes of members. Christian virtues of industry and thrift made the sum total of offerings of even the humblest laboring members a sizable one. Most of their earnings, over and above the necessities of food, clothing and shelter, and taxation, went to the church; for Christians had few social and cultural demands of importance outside their fellowship. Regarded from purely practical considerations the church served the ordinary member as an insurance society against sickness, unemployment, imprisonment, or death.

Some idea of the expanding capital of the church as it grew in numbers may be gained from the fact that as early as the year 144 the church in Rome paid back to an expelled Gnostic named Marcion the sum of $8,000 which he had contributed from his shipping business. By the third century the churches were beginning to acquire extensive properties—on what legal basis is unknown—and to count in their numbers members of the emperors' families, the wealthiest household of the Empire. One of Valerian's principal measures in attempting to destroy Christianity in 257 was the confiscation of all property owned by Christians individually or collectively. In the generation following Valerian Christianity grew enormously in economic prestige.

Cultural development.—The early Christians tended to despise the wisdom of this world as foolishness in the sight of God. True, many of the early leaders, like Paul, were men of fair education; but such learning as they had was acquired before they became Christians. So concerned were Christians with the imminent coming of the kingdom and preaching the good news of Jesus that they scarcely gave any thought to education, save for the study of the Scriptures for moral examples and proofs of Jesus' fulfilment of prophecy. By the turn of the second century the need began to be felt for a defense of Christian faith to the more thoughtful elements of society, who were begininng to take some interest in the movement. We have already noted in this regard the work of the apologists, who attempted to utilize salient items of gentile philosophy in explaining Christian beliefs and morals. An added service was rendered by the apologists' "schools" in refuting the opinions of the Gnostics and other purveyors of unorthodox doctrines.

In order to protect itself from receiving members inadequately prepared for a Christian life, the church developed in the second half of the second century a system known as the catechumenate. This was a course of instruction, normally covering three years' study and preparatory to baptism, designed to test the fitness of converts from paganism. The subjects treated in the catechetical classes included the "creed," with a refutation of pagan religious beliefs and practices, the Scriptures, and Christian morals.

Most famous of all the catechetical schools was the one in Alexandria, founded about the year 180. This school developed into what one might call a Christian university. The first headmasters, Pantaenus and his pupil Clement, were distinguished men of letters and culture, who were converted to Christianity as being the "true" philosophy. Not only did they train new converts to the faith but they offered advance courses of study to those desiring a comprehensive and exhaustive knowledge of the Scriptures. The Alexandrian school was famous for its development of the "allegorical" exposition of Scripture, a method of interpretation widely used by Greek-speaking Jews and Stoic philosophers. It aimed at discovering the hidden, spiritual meaning of any given passage of Scripture underneath its plain and literal meaning.

Clement's successor as head of the school was a youth of eighteen years, Origen, the son of a Christian martyr, and a lad of extraordinary vitality and zest for learning. Above all, Origen possessed one of the saintliest and purest characters known in all Christian history. The fruits of his encyclopedic reading and study were published in literally thousands of books. Origen studied Hebrew and produced a monumental edition of the Bible in its Hebrew and Greek texts. He was the first person who formulated and wrote a complete system of Christian theology, his book *On First Principles.* We have already had occasion to mention his great apology *Against Celsus.* Among pagan thinkers, equally as among Christians, he enjoyed the greatest reputation. The later years of his life were spent in Caesarea in Palestine, where he died in 253 from the effects of torture endured in the persecution of Decius. In the work of Origen one may say without exaggeration that Christianity's conquest of the intellectual life of the ancient world was assured.

CHAPTER II

CHRISTIANITY AND THE FALL
OF ROME

5. CHRISTIANITY AS A STATE RELIGION

Constantine.—The edict of toleration granted the Christians by the dying Galerius was an admission of failure of persecution to destroy the religion of Jesus. In the western provinces of the Empire the policy of repression had never had more than half-hearted support from the co-rulers of Diocletian and Galerius. The new emperor, Constantine, was genuinely sympathetic to Christianity as well as anxious to secure the support of the Christian population for his regime. Accordingly, in 313 he induced his eastern colleague to issue with him an edict granting the Christians full legal standing on the same basis as all other religions in the Empire and restoration of all their properties out of the public treasury.

Constantine believed that the Christian God had assisted him in winning his battles for control of the Empire, and he therefore desired a continuance of whatever divine help the Christian religion might afford in maintaining the peace and welfare of his rule. The political wisdom of his policy was amply vindicated in the extravagant devotion and loyalty which he received from his Christian subjects. Constantine's own

33

personal religion is a subject of speculation. He was not baptized until his deathbed. This much can be said with assurance: (1) his intervention in religious affairs was in large measure dictated by what he considered to be politically expedient and (2) from the beginning of his reign he increasingly identified himself with the church, took a commanding interest in its internal affairs, and finally in the later years of his life openly called upon his subjects to give up paganism.

The emperor placed Christian symbols on his coins and on the standards and shields of his troops and removed his own image from pagan temples. Full civil rights were given the churches, the Christian clergy were exempted from taxation, and pagan officials were expressly forbidden to interfere with Christians for refusing to participate in public sacrifices. Moneys were given the Christians to build churches; in Rome several large public buildings were turned over to them for use as sanctuaries. In 325 Constantine began the foundation of his new capital, the city of Constantinople, as a definitely Christian metropolis, to supersede old pagan Rome. At the same time he forbade state functionaries to offer sacrifices in official pagan ceremonies.

As supreme head of the state in all causes civil and religious Constantine had no hesitancy in interfering in internal disputes in the church to establish peace and punish offenders. As early as the year 314 he attempted, unsuccessfully, to heal a schism in the churches of North Africa. A group known as Donatists had rejected the validity of ordination of the bishop of Carthage, and other clergy, whom they accused of betraying sacred properties in the Diocletian persecution. A council of bishops held in Arles decided against the Donatists. For several years Constantine tried to enforce by confiscation and even death the decisions of the council, but repression only strengthened the Donatist cause. For over a hundred years the Donatist churches maintained a vigorous, and at times dominant, activity in the religious life of North Africa.

The Council of Nicaea.—In 325 Constantine summoned all the bishops throughout the Empire to meet at Nicaea, in Asia Minor, to settle an acrimonious doctrinal dispute which had arisen in the church in Alexandria and which was assuming ever larger proportions as bishops in the eastern provinces ranged themselves on one side or the other. The occasion of the controversy was the preaching of Arius, a devout and learned presbyter of the Alexandrian church. Arius maintained that Christ, the Son of God, was created by and subordinate to God the Father, and hence was not eternal. At the same time, Christ was more than a man and the fitting object of worship. Bishop Alexander excommunicated Arius for these opinions, asserting that Christ was fully divine as much as God the Father and also that he was a complete and perfect man.

Arius' cause was at once taken up by Bishop Eusebius of Nicomedia, a prelate of enormous ambition and little moral scruple, who immediately fanned the flame of debate so as to spread far beyond the confines of Alexandria. Leadership of the opponents of Arius was taken by Bishop Alexander's young deacon, Athanasius (who succeeded as bishop three years later, 328). About three hundred bishops attended the gathering at Nicaea, over which Constantine himself presided. The position of Arius was utterly rejected, and he with several loyal companions was deposed and banished. The council would have then disbanded except for the resolute determination of a small party led by Athanasius to have the bishops draw up an authoritative definition of the church's faith. The result was the so-called Nicene Creed.

This creed asserted that God the Father was Creator of all that is, visible and invisible, that Jesus Christ, his only begotten Son, was "very God of very God," of the same divine essence as God the Father, who for our salvation was incarnated in human flesh and became man. Constantine felt gratified that peace was at last established in the church. His confidence was soon to be rudely shaken. The council was but a prelude to a bitter struggle which convulsed the church for over half a century.

Doctrinal controversy.—The disastrous policy inaugurated by Constantine of imposing the decisions of church councils by force came to full fruition after his death in 337. His son Constantius sympathized with the Arian cause; as a consequence, bishops who adhered faithfully to the Nicene Creed were banished. Strife seemed endless, as first one side and then the other succeeded in winning support of the emperors. For example, Athanasius was banished from his bishopric in Alexandria five different times. Innumerable councils were summoned by the emperors, and various creeds put forth as compromises. Neither side, however, trusted the good faith of the other, and all attempts at mediation were rendered futile by the emperors' constant threat of force.

The churches of the western provinces, now almost entirely Latin-speaking, had no great interest in the controversy; though they generally favored the party of Athanasius. In the eastern provinces the Arians themselves split into several rival camps and so weakened their position. A combination of force and persuasion finally produced a triumph for the faith of Nicaea, at a council in Constantinople in 381 under the emperor Theodosius I. The creed adopted at this council reaffirmed the statements of the Nicene Creed but dropped the anathemas against the Arians. A considerable section was added about the Holy Spirit—"who together with the Father and the Son is worshiped and glorified."

No sooner was the Arian controversy settled than another fierce doctrinal controversy developed regarding the exact character of the union of divine and human natures in Christ. Two solutions were offered: one by the leading theologians of Syria and the other by a party headed successively by the bishops of Alexandria. The former group, represented by Nestorius, an Antiochene who became bishop of Constantinople, declared that Christ had both a divine and a human nature, perfectly united in one person by the complete accord of their respective divine and human wills.

The Alexandrian party, led by Bishop Cyril, tended to emphasize the absorption of Christ's human nature by his divine nature and accused the Nestorians of splitting the personality of Christ, so to speak. Actually both parties greatly exaggerated their disagreements in doctrine. Underlying the conflict was an unmitigated spirit of jealousy, partisanship and envy, and the rivalry of large churches for dominant influence.

Numerous councils invoked by the emperors to settle the dispute were marked by disorder and an utter lack of Christian charity, and they ultimately destroyed the unity of Christendom. Cyril succeeded in getting Nestorius condemned at a council in Ephesus in 431: and a large proportion of the Syrian churches followed Nestorius into schism. But twenty years later, at a council in Chalcedon (in Asia Minor, across from Constantinople), Cyril's party met a decisive defeat. The creed adopted by this council, largely through the influence of Leo the Great, bishop of Rome, declared that Jesus Christ was one person in whom a completely divine and completely human nature were inseparably and unconfusedly united. Most of the Egyptian churches refused to accept the decision of Chalcedon and separated from communion with the "orthodox" church. The disunion of Christianity created by these bitter doctrinal quarrels has never yet been healed.

The end of paganism.—The policy of toleration of all religions in the Empire was not continued by Constantine's sons and successors. Laws were passed abolishing pagan sacrifices and closing the temples. These were not strictly enforced, however, particularly in areas remaining predominantly pagan. Theoretically, at least, the emperor continued to be the official head of the state religion as of former times. Because of imperial favor to the church, the number of Christians grew rapidly. Many who sought baptism, of course, had no strong convictions in favor of Christianity but allowed themselves to be carried by the general trend of the times for reasons of political or social advantage. In many localities crowds of fanatic and zealous Christians actually set upon the destruction of pagan sanctuaries with impunity. In other places Christians were permitted to take over properties of pagan cults which had fallen into dilapidation from disuse.

In the brief reign of the emperor Julian (361–63) a strenuous effort was made to reverse the declining fortunes of paganism. Julian possessed a sensitive, poetic nature, enamored with the traditional mythologies and ceremonies of the ancient cults. He was an avid student of Greek literature and philosophy, a pursuit more congenial to his temperament than the hair-splitting arguments over doctrine of his Christian teachers. Accordingly, when he came to the throne, he resolved to restore pagan worship to its ancient splendor. The temples were reopened, and properties confiscated by Christians given back to their former uses. All privileges granted the Christian clergy were revoked. Christians were excluded from public office and commands in the army and from all professorships in public schools. Plans were set for an elaborate organization of revived paganism, modeled on that of the church. Julian's sudden death in a war campaign against Persia brought to an end his hopes.

Julian's religious policy was doomed to failure in any event. His religion was that of a scholar and student, out of touch with the real condition of paganism. Its utter lack of sympathy with the austere moral demands which Julian endeavored to inject into it showed the true principle of its inevitable decay. Julian's successors renewed the policy of the sons of Constantine. A party of pagan senators in Rome made a valiant endeavor to ward off repressive measures; but all their attempts were thwarted by the vigilance of an able bishop in Milan, Ambrose, who enjoyed a great reputation with the emperors for his stalwart character and exceptional abilities in both civil and church affairs. In 392 Theodosius I gave the death knell to paganism by outlawing its public and private practice as a crime of lese majesty. Henceforth Christianity was the only legal religion of the Empire.

The external and internal transformation in the life of the church during the fourth century was enormous. The bishops became high dignitaries of the state and were granted extensive powers as magistrates in civil and judicial affairs. They supervised all agencies of poor relief and charitable institutions, such as hospitals, orphanages, and hostels. By gift or bequest they administered immense holdings in property for the upkeep of imposing church edifices, the support of numerous clergy, and the endowment of their charities. The worship of the churches became elaborate and splendid. It was an age of great preachers, most noted of whom were Bishop Ambrose in Milan (d. 397) and Bishop John in Constantinople, named Chrysostom (the "Golden-mouthed"). The latter's fiery denunciations of the morals of the empress led to his downfall, and he died in exile in 407. The numerous councils which met to debate doctrinal issues brought all sections of the church into intimate contact with one another. They served not only to formulate authoritative standards of dogma but also to regularize diverse local traditions and customs of discipline and worship into a common code of church law, recognized and observed by all Christian communities.

6. CHRISTIAN MONASTICISM

Sources of monasticism.—It has often been noted by students of Christian history that the true successors of the martyrs were the monks. It is certainly not a coincidence that the fourth century, which witnessed the church's peace with the secular world, saw the rise and development of monasticism in Christianity. There was an inevitable lowering of the average standards of devotion and morality attendant upon the influx of society generally into the Christian fold when it became the favored religion of the state and no longer subject to the threat of persecution.

Yet it would be a great mistake to regard the growth of monasticism in the fourth century as solely due to the protest of more ardent religious spirits against the current trend toward secularization of Christianity by its intermixture in worldly affairs. The fundamental religious ground of the monastic life is the renunciation of earthly, material values for the sake of more intangible, spiritual goods. Its morality is the discipline of the cody and its wants (called in Greek *askesis*, whence the word "ascetic"), so that the soul may be as free as possible to serve purely religious ends.

We have noted in a previous section that many Christians during the first three centuries adopted a life of virginity and celibacy in reaction to the low standards of sexual morality with which they were familiar in the gentile world. With this fact must be associated the widespread opinion among many religious people in ancient times, both Christian and non-Christian, that the material world was essentially evil and the way of salvation was to escape as far as possible from concern and entanglement with its responsibilities and pleasures. Public affairs, private wealth, marriage, even the quest for food and clothing were considered burdens which drew the attention of the soul away from its native task of prayer and contemplation of the unseen and eternally rewarding riches of God.

Such a mood was ready to take quite literally the saying of Jesus that one must forsake everything earthly to obtain the Kingdom of Heaven. By the third century Christian "virgins" were counted in sufficient numbers to be recognized as a distinct order in the church. Many women ascetics took vows of lifelong celibacy and received from the bishop a symbolic veiling as a sign of their separation from the world. Where possible they lived together under the supervision of a widow or matron. Their daily life was devoted to fasting, prayer, and works of mercy. Fellow-Christians held them in high esteem.

Early monasticism in Egypt.—About the year 285 an Egyptian named Antony left a comfortable and well-to-do home to retire into solitude in the desert. There he practiced an extremely austere life, eating once a day a simple fare of bread, salt, and water, sleeping little, spending his time in prayer and in combat with demons who seemed to him to haunt the place. Antony attracted many admirers and imitators. During the fourth century literally thousands of Christians took up their abode in the Egyptian deserts, many of them as solitaries, but many more in a semiorganized fashion under the leadership of masters of the ascetic life.

The monks lived in caves or small huts, singly or in twos and threes, and assembled together in large congregations only on Saturdays and Sundays for services of worship and instruction. The feats of fasting and abstinence which they endured seem almost incredible to the modern man; for example, some ate only once a week. Most of the monks were illiterate, but all of them learned by heart much of the Scriptures and meditated on them day and night. In order to procure the slight needs of sustenance for bare bodily existence in the warm climate of Egypt, some engaged in agriculture and others wove baskets and mats for sale in the markets. All received gifts from the numbers of pilgrims who came to visit them and witness their struggles to master temptation.

On an island in the Upper Nile, Tabennisi, a former

soldier named Pachomius (d. 345) organized a large group of monks for the first time into a definite communal life under a fixed rule. The huts where the monks slept were inclosed within a wall. All the monks ate in a common refectory and participated in daily morning and evening services of worship. Manual labor of various sorts was prescribed and income for the monastery provided by the sale of its products. Strict obedience to the head of the monastery, the abbot, was required in all matters pertaining to the life of the community. Novices were subjected to a careful period of probation to test their fitness for membership in the monastery. Pachomius established eight monasteries and supervised several convents of nuns, some of which were founded by his sister.

Spread of monasticism.—Almost simultaneously with the developments in Egypt, monasticism made its appearance in Palestine and Syria. In these regions it often took bizarre forms, such as the case of the well-known Simeon Stylites (385–459), who lived for years on top of a high pillar from which he preached to the crowds gathered to watch him. Considerable rivalry was developed among these ascetics in attempts to break records of self-discipline.

A moderate and sane system of monastic regulation was the work of Basil of Caesarea in Cappadocia. Reared in an illustrious and devout family, Basil received an excellent education in the famed University of Athens. Largely through the influence of his sister, he determined to devote his life to religion. The monastic vocation made a strong appeal to him, and he decided to visit the ascetic communities in Egypt to gain firsthand acquaintance with their method and spirit. Returning to his native land, he devoted himself to ascetic retirement in a beautiful site on the river Iris, near a similar retreat of his mother and sister. Companions gathered, and a monastery was established. Basil's exceptional talents in administration and theological learning engaged him increasingly in affairs of church and state, and in 370 he was selected to be bishop of Caesarea, a position he held until his death in 379. Among other things, he was a persuasive advocate of orthodox doctrine and had much influence in reconciling moderate Arians to the faith of Nicaea.

Basil's numerous ascetical writings have become the basis of monastic life and organization throughout eastern Christian lands. He favored a communal life for monks as a more wholesome atmosphere for moral and spiritual health than the hermit life so prevalent in Egypt. He was strongly indebted to the Pachomian system of organization and encouraged the establishlishment of monasteries in close proximity to cities where they could exert a stronger influence upon the religious life of the church. His rules provided for eight daily periods of common worship. The remainder of the monks' waking hours was to be spent in manual labor or other useful work, such as the education of children. Basil disapproved of excessive austerities and stressed instead the more temperate and sociable virtues of scriptural teaching.

The Egyptian monastic movement was brought to the attention of the Western Latin-speaking Christians by visits of Athanasius during his periods of banishment from Alexandria, when he was accompanied by several loyal monks. Athanasius was keenly interested in the movement and wrote a life of Antony which was widely read and which is still extant. In Rome many ladies of great wealth and position turned their homes into nunneries. Their chief preceptor in asceticism came to be a noted scholar, Jerome (340–420), whose prodigious learning was matched only by his fanatic enthusiasm for monasticism. Jerome induced several high-born ladies to follow him to Palestine, where they established neighboring monasteries near the holy sites of Bethlehem. In these sacred surroundings Jerome carried on exhaustive scholarly research, translated the Scriptures from Hebrew and Greek into stately Latin (the Vulgate version), and engaged in many discussions of theology and morals with other students and writers, oftentimes in a bitter and uncharitable manner.

Western monasticism.—In Gaul (modern France) two important centers of monasticism developed at this period. The earlier one was inspired by Martin (d. 397), who deserted a promising career in the army to become a hermit. His fame attracted many disciples and ultimately forced him, unwillingly, to become bishop of Tours. The caves of his monks are still to be seen at Marmoutier, near Tours, where he established his monastery much after the fashion of the Egyptian ascetics. On the southern coast of Gaul a flourishing group of monasteries was founded at the turn of the fifth century, notably on the island of Lérins (in 410) and in the city of Marseilles. The latter was the work of John Cassian, who made extensive visits to the monastic settlements in Egypt and published about the year 425 his interviews with the Egyptian masters of ascetic life. These writings of Cassian, known as the *Institutes* and *Conferences*, exercised a wide influence upon the development of Western monasticism throughout the Middle Ages. In Lérins and Marseilles were trained the major leaders of the church in Gaul for over a hundred years and also many missionaries and monastic founders of the distant isles of Britain and Ireland.

Little is known of the early monastic developments in Italy. Leading bishops recommended the movement, and presumably many Christians devoted their lives to ascetic retirement, either as solitaries or as loosely organized communities. Not until the first half of the sixth century did there arise a genius to give stability to the movement. By that time social and political conditions had greatly altered, due to the fall of Roman imperial power in western Europe and an ensuing period of disorder in affairs of church and state. (This situation will be dealt with in the next section.) During this era of change two great names stand out in the story of monastic organization in the West.

One is Cassiodorus (d. 573). After a distinguished career of forty years in government service he retired to a monastery at Vivarium in southern Italy. A noted man of letters himself, Cassiodorus enlisted his monks in the study and preservation of literature. To this end he gathered at Vivarium a magnificent library of manuscripts. To the influence of his example is due much of the credit for the conservation of ancient learning by monasticism during the centuries of social chaos and ignorance in western Europe.

Contemporary with Cassiodorus was Benedict, a native of the little town of Nursia. Leaving the university at Rome, where his well-to-do parents had sent him, Benedict fled from what he felt were evil associations to a life of solitude in the Italian hills. After two unsuccessful attempts at governing monasteries which sought him out to be their abbot, he finally settled with some companions at Monte Cassino, an old fortress located midway between Rome and Naples. Here Benedict remained until his death (*ca.* 550) and wrote for his monks the *Rule* which has made him deservedly famous as the "father" of Western monasticism.

The *Rule* was not marked by any original or novel character. It depends much upon the work of Pachomius, Basil, Cassian, and others. But its moderation and good sense have commended it to succeeding generations of monastic founders. Benedict's personal experiences taught him the unwisdom of individualistic, undisciplined asceticism. Besides poverty and chastity, the basic virtue of the monk lay in humility and strict obedience to the abbot. Each monastery was an independent unit and elected its own abbot, who exercised for life an absolute authority. The abbot himself should be a wise father to his household; and certainly much of the success of the Benedictine system was dependent upon his character. The monks ate and slept in a common room. Their entire daily life was carefully regulated in periods of worship, labor, and study. From Basil the eight times of common worship were adopted, and Benedict outlined carefully their order of service in psalms, hymns, prayers, and Scripture reading. Except for necessary business of the community, monks were not allowed to leave the monastery. Thus Benedict gave to monasticism an orderly government and discipline, derived from the best experience of two hundred years of the movement, which served the church in "the dark ages" as models of Christian society and community life.

7. The Church Meets the Barbarian Invasions

The fall of Rome.—When Theodosius I died in 395, the Roman Empire was divided between his sons, never to be reunited. Fifteen years later the city of Rome was sacked by Alaric, king of the Goths. These early years of the fifth century saw the entire western half of the Empire overrun with barbarian Germanic tribes, who at last had shattered the frontier defenses which for centuries had held them out of the bounds of Roman civilization. After ransacking Italy the Goths passed on to southern Gaul and ultimately took up permanent settlement in Spain. Before they arrived, Gaul and Spain had been overwhelmed by waves of Alans, Vandals, and Sueves. The Vandals, in turn, pushed by the Goths, crossed over into North Africa, where in short order they made themselves masters. Meanwhile, the Anglo-Saxons began to attack and settle the British Isles, and the Franks started a series of conquests which was to lay most of Gaul at their feet before the end of the century.

To make confusion worse confounded these Germanic peoples considered themselves as allies of the Empire and frequently joined forces with the imperial army against one another. Certainly the barbarians had no thought of destroying the Empire. They never conceived of a world without it! Their main interest was in plunder, and having satisfied themselves with material wealth and sensual pleasures they settled down on the large country estates in fairly tolerable relations with their Roman neighbors.

The military failure of the Empire was a direct result of a gradual decay in its political and economic health, which had set in as early as the third century and had only been delayed by the energetic reforms of Diocletian and Constantine. Briefly stated, the rich were getting richer, and the poor poorer. Repressive taxation to support a top-heavy machinery of government and defense had laid heavy toll on the middle class. Cities declined, as rich and poor alike retired to country landholdings less easily accessible to the tax-gatherer. Large landed proprietors tended to take under their protection small farmers in return for regular services, thus reducing numbers of folk to virtual serfdom. The invasions only reinforced this trend toward "feudalism." The center of economy shifted from the city to the rural village of the large estates; hence commerce became of little consequence. Culturally there was marked decline. The barbarians had no interest in education, and economic conditions rendered the old system of state schools impossible.

Effect on the church.—The immediate effect of the fall of the Empire in the West was an extreme pessimism. The world seemed crumbling to ruins. Old Roman families who still clung to paganism openly charged that the adoption of Christianity by the state was the cause of disaster. The gods were wreaking vengeance for men's desertion of them. The church met the challenge of events with remarkable courage and energy. Her answer to the new situation was decisively given in the *City of God*, written by one of the greatest thinkers of all time, Augustine, bishop of Hippo in North Africa.

Augustine was born in 354 of a pious Christian mother and a prosperous and kindly pagan father. He received an excellent education and turned to a career of teaching rhetoric and philosophy, successively in Carthage, Rome, and Milan. In his *Confessions* he has left a luminous account of his inner religious struggles which finally led him to accept baptism from Bishop Ambrose of Milan in 387. Augustine returned to Africa in the hope of spending his days in quiet study of philosophy and theology; but his extraordinary personal and intellectual gifts marked him out for active leadership in the church. As a bishop Augustine turned his attention particularly to defending the church and its teaching from calumnies of heretics and pagans. In this task his candor, charity, and learning combined to assure him lasting success. For example, he was largely responsible for bringing to naught the influence of the Donatists in North Africa. Christian thinking owes an immeasurable debt to Augustine even in modern times.

In the *City of God*, mentioned above, Augustine argued that the chances and changes which befall the temporal state cannot upset the ultimate destiny which God in his providence is preparing for his church. The sack of Rome was a just reward for its sins of the past. In the long run of history righteousness will prevail and the earthly city in which men live will be transformed by the heavenly city of God where is the true habitation of faithful men. Having left this legacy of hope, Augustine died in 430 while the Vandals were laying siege to his episcopal city of Hippo.

Throughout the Western church bishops gave courageous leadership to their flock in facing the invaders. Sometimes they organized the defense of their cities; at other times they treated with the barbarian chieftains for satisfactory terms. The churches were turned into asylums and hospitals for refugees and more than once provided havens of safety for the population because of the barbarians' superstitious fear of sacred places. Schools were established in cathedrals and monasteries, where candidates for the ministry might obtain a modicum of education, at least. After the fifth century literacy was largely confined to the clergy. As a consequence, the barbarian rulers depended upon the bishops and learned monks as counselors and officers of such civil administration as existed. In this way the church served as the conservor and custodian of whatever survived of the old culture and became the chief medium of reconciliation between the native and invading peoples in the rise of a new social order in western Europe.

Conversion of the barbarians.—Of prime significance for the future of Europe was the success of the church in bringing the Germanic peoples into the fold of the Catholic church. Before their entrance into the Roman Empire many of the barbarian tribes had been evangelized by Arian missionaries, foremost of whom was Ulfilas (d. 383). Ulfilas had been consecrated as a bishop for the Goths in 341. During his work among them he translated the Bible and the liturgy into their vernacular tongue. From the Goths Arian Christianity passed to other tribes, notably the Vandals, Sueves, and Burgundians.

During the invasions the barbarians set up their own churches under their tribal bishops side by side with the Latin-speaking, Catholic churches of the Romans. Some friction between the two organizations was inevitable. Yet only the Vandals were active persecutors of Catholicism. In North Africa they confiscated the Catholic churches, drove the bishops and clergy into exile, and ruthlessly oppressed loyal Catholic layfolk. The result was disastrous for the future of Christianity in this region. The persecution so weakened the church in North Africa that it was unable to withstand the onslaught of Mohammedan Saracens who swept across the territory in the conquests of the seventh century. Thus North Africa was lost to Christianity until our own times.

In Spain and Italy, where the Goths were masters,

the Roman population not only was allowed to practice its religion unmolested but was also permitted to enjoy its own civil laws. In Italy a remarkable degree of order and justice was maintained by the Gothic king Theodoric (493–526). Among his chief ministers of state were two eminent men of letters: Cassiodorus, whom we have already met, and the philosopher Boethius, author of a classic of literature, *The Consolations of Philosophy*. After Theodoric's death the emperor Justinian I (527–65) sought to restore imperial authority in Italy and also in North Africa. In a long and devastating war he did succeed in crushing the Goths and Vandals. But he so exhausted these territories that Italy was laid open to fresh invasion by the savage Lombards, and Africa was ultimately lost to the Saracens.

The Frankish invaders of Gaul were pagans. Under their cunning and treacherous king Clovis (d. 511) they gained control of the northern and central portions of the province; and in the sixth century they extended their sway over the Burgundian kingdom in the southeast and curbed the power of the Goths north of the Pyrenees. Clovis with characteristic shrewdness submitted to the pressure of his Catholic queen to receive baptism in 496; for he realized that the Catholic church would be a powerful ally for the Franks, both against the Arians (Burgundians and Goths) and in the pacification of the Roman populations of his own territories. His people loyally followed him en masse into the church. In 589 the Goths in Spain joined their Frankish neighbors by renouncing Arianism and entering the Catholic fold. The significance of these decisions was tremendous. It meant that the political divisions and disruptive social forces incident upon the Germanic settlement in the Empire would not be reinforced by separate national churches. The Latin, Catholic church could give western Europe such unity as it was able to enjoy for centuries to come; and, with the support of an aggressive people like the Franks, it could transmit to the new peoples something of the civilization and ideals which Christianity inherited from the Roman Empire.

During these centuries of chaotic social change, the church pushed its evangelizing work into the rural areas, which under the old empire had been little touched by Christianity. On all the great landed estates, whether owned by the church or by noble landlords, parish churches were built and clergy instituted to serve the village and country folk, including both native Romans and barbarian settlers. Many quarrels were engendered as to who should have control of the appointments and revenues of these parishes, the bishop or the landlord who provided the building. A compromise was usually reached, whereby the owner of the parish property had the right to nominate the parish priest, the bishop to approve and institute him. The bishop's share of the parish revenues was limited to one-fourth; and he was required to visit annually all the parishes within his diocese or send a deputy, usually his archdeacon. The boundaries of the dioceses generally followed the old Roman districts of civil administration. Theoretically the bishops were chosen by the clergy of their cathedral churches in the cities where they resided. Actually, there was an increasing tendency toward interference by the king in their appointment, since much of their time was taken by affairs of state.

The papacy.—The greatest prestige was enjoyed by the bishop of Rome, commonly called the pope. From early times the popes claimed to be a final court of appeal on all questions of doctrine and discipline arising in the church by virtue of the alleged foundation of their church by Peter, the chief of Christ's apostles. Actually, such authority as they exercised depended upon a variety of circumstances—political conditions in Italy and other provinces, interference by the emperor in Constantinople, and the moral force of character of individual popes. On doctrinal issues the popes generally represented the entire Latin church and stoutly resisted efforts of the emperors to compromise their orthodoxy by formulas designed to procure religious peace in the eastern provinces.

Problems of discipline and worship were frequently referred to the popes by bishops and councils all over the West. To these the popes responded sometimes in the spirit of counsel, sometimes with the note of command. Locally in Italy the popes assumed an effective leadership in resisting the depredations of the barbarians, notably the Lombards, upon the church, and in organizing the relief of the populace from war, pestilence, and famine. A keen interest was taken in all efforts to convert the barbarians to Catholicism, and letters of exhortation were addressed to secular and

ecclesiastical leaders to reform abuses and prevent en-
croachments upon the privileges of the church and its
properties. Most successful of all the popes in enhanc-
ing the prestige of the papacy during these centuries
were Leo the Great (440–61) and Gregory the Great
(590–604). The writings of the latter, including his
commentaries on Job (the *Moralia*), the *Pastoral Rule*,
and a collection of stories of saints called *Dialogues*,
effectively transmitted to the rude society of the times
the elemental teaching of the church in matters of
faith and morals and to a great extent molded the
piety of Christians for generations to come.

8. EVANGELIZATION OF THE BRITISH ISLES

Roman Britain.—The British Isles were never completely subject to the Roman Empire. Ireland and the
highlands of Scotland always lay outside its frontier.
The native peoples of the islands comprised two families of the Celtic race: the Goidels or Irish and the
Britons and an older, possibly non-Celtic race of Picts
who inhabited the north of Scotland. Only the Britons, therefore, were brought to any extent under the
influence of Roman civilization, with cities and towns
as the centers of political and commercial activity and
with Latin as the language af society and culture. During the fourth century the Empire's military control of
Britain began to weaken, and in the early years of the
fifth century all Roman troops were withdrawn to the
Continent for use against the Germanic invaders.
Britain was left to defend itself against forays of Irish
marauders from the west, Picts from the north, and

Germans from the east. For early in the fifth century the Germanic tribes of Angles and Saxons began to attack and settle the island.

Christian missionaries had reached Britain by the end of the second century; but little is known of British Christianity until the fourth century. Several British martyrs suffered in the persecution of Diocletian, and three British bishops attended the Council of Arles in 314 which investigated the Donatist schism. Archeologists have uncovered remains of several fourth-century churches in Britain; and by the end of the century the territory of the island within the boundaries of the Empire was predominantly Christian. There is nothing to show that the organization and life of the church in Britain differed from that on the Continent.

Conversion of Ireland.—In an Irish raid on the west coast of Britain about the year 400 a sixteen-year-old lad named Patrick was carried off into captivity. Six years later Patrick made his escape. But he had not returned home for long before he had a vision calling him to missionary service in the land of his former masters. He proceeded to Gaul to prepare himself for the task; and in 432 was sent as a bishop to Ireland. Doubtless there were already many Christians scattered throughout Ireland among the slaves or those who had family or commercial connections with Britain or the Continent. To Patrick, however, is due the honor of planting the church firmly on Irish soil.

Beginning his work in Ulster, the place of his former captivity, Patrick covered most of northern Ireland in his missionary journeys, not without considerable risk to his life from the machinations of the heathen wise men, or druids. His method of operation seems generally to have been to win over tribal chieftains to the faith, who would in turn grant him a parcel of land for a church. The chief king of all Ireland stoutly refused to be converted, but Patrick won over his brother and two of his daughters. By the time of his death in 461 the work of evangelization was well under way, and several bishops were assisting in the mission.

The next hundred years witnessed the complete Christianization of Ireland. Details of this expansion are obscure; but there was a good deal of intercommunication with the Christians of Britain, who during this period were steadily pushed by the Anglo-Saxons to the western parts of the island, chiefly the hill country of Wales. Thus cut off from easy access to Continental Christianity, the Irish and Welsh (or British) developed a form of church organization peculiarly adapted to the political and social customs of the Celtic peoples.

Celtic Christianity.—The Celts were organized as clans (or tribes), whose members claimed at least a theoretical kinship and whose chieftains were elected from among the older men of the "family." They lived in scattered agricultural communities and counted their wealth principally in the form of livestock. Plunder and warfare among the clans was a common diversion. Strangers had no rights unless they were adopted into a clan. Churches were endowed by allotments of land and livestock from the common property of the clan or by gift of some Christian clansman.

Invariably they developed into monasteries, as men or women associated themselves with the founders in devotion to a distinctly religious life.

The churches or monasteries took their name from the founder, who was called a saint, and the members of his religious house were called the family of the saint. The head or abbot of the monastery might be a bishop or a presbyter. In Ireland he was usually a presbyter; in Wales, a bishop. In any case, each monastery included one person who had the rank of bishop, and sometimes there were several bishops connected with a house. Their functions were purely spiritual, for ordinations, confirmations, consecration of churches, etc. The government of the monastery lay solely in the hands of the abbot. Moreover, the abbotship passed as a rule by inheritance to a near kinsman of the abbot; though occasionally outsiders were elected, Daughter-monasteries were founded when the abbot gave permission to one or more of his monks to settle elsewhere. But every monastery was completely self-governing and followed its own rules of discipline and worship.

The monks lived in separate wattle huts within a walled inclosure. Discipline was exceedingly strict. Much allowance was made for individual austerities, which at times assumed extravagant proportions. A rude stone or wattle church was used for the customary eight daily services of common worship and also served as a parish church for the neighboring village. Many of the monasteries became famous as centers of learning and study of the Scriptures. Numbers of students even came from distant lands to receive instruction from Irish masters. Fees were paid in kind. Manuscripts were highly prized, as parchment was scarce. The Irish had amazing intellectual curiosity and were fond of indulging in recondite and enigmatic problems. Some monks dabbled in Greek. Their mastery of Latin was amazing, if inclined to be bookish and ornamented with strange words and queer spellings.

Wanderlust has characterized the Irish in all ages —reinforced by economic necessity and religious devotion. Monks literally swarmed like bees from Ireland to Britain and the Continent during the sixth, seventh, and eighth centuries. Some of the most famous monasteries of the Continent in the Middle Ages were founded by Irish *émigrés*. The Welsh also, to a less extent, wandered abroad. To them is due the Christianization of Brittany in Gaul. Though the independent and individualistic temper of the Irish made them a nuisance to the secular and ecclesiastical authorities of the localities where they settled their ascetic devotion and abundant learning contributed immensely toward improving the tone of religious life in areas suffering from the disruptive effects of the barbarian invasions.

The Irish were zealous missionaries. Oftentimes a monk left his home to work among the heathen as a penance for his sins. Such was the occasion in 563 of the planting of Christianity in Scotland by Columba, a man of royal blood and founder of several noted monasteries in Ireland. With twelve companions Columba settled on the small island of Iona off the west coast of Scotland. Earlier mission work had been carried on in southern Scotland from the monastery of Whitern, founded in the early fifth century by a British disciple of Martin of Tours named Ninian. Columba's foundation at Iona spread the gospel among the Irish who settled in Argyll, beginning about the year 500, and among the Picts of the highlands. The Iona monks also took a leading rôle in the conversion of the Anglo-Saxons.

Conversion of the English.—All vestiges of Christianity were destroyed by the pagan Anglo-Saxons, or English, in the territories conquered by them from the British. The implacable hostility of the two peoples blocked any thought of mission work by the British among their enemies. Nor did the Franks take any interest in evangelizing their neighbors across the Channel, although intermarriage and trade relations between them and the English were common. The initiative for the conversion of the English came from Rome, where the appearance of several English youths on the slave market fired the imagination of Pope Gregory the Great with the hope of winning them to the Christian faith. Favorable political relations between the pope and the Frankish rulers opened the way in 596, and Gregory dispatched a party of Benedictine monks, headed by one Augustine, with letters to important Frankish leaders, both secular and ecclesiastical, asking their assistance to the missionary project.

Augustine and his monks were respectfully received by the English king residing in Canterbury, for his queen was a Christian Frankish princess. Setting up the headquarters of their mission at Canterbury, Augustine repaired to Gaul for consecration as archbishop of the English. The English king accepted baptism. With his encouragement the mission work expanded, and bishops were instituted in Rochester and London. A marriage alliance with a northern English king opened the way to missionary work in the region around York. These initial successes in Christianization were offset in a short time by strong pagan reactions which forced the bishops of London, and later of York, to flee for their lives. The British Christians in Wales absolutely refused to co-operate with the Roman missionaries and even allied themselves with pagan English tribes in wars against the Christian English.

At this point the Irish monks of Iona were invited to start work among the northern English by a young king who had spent several years of exile in refuge at the monastery. In typical Irish fashion the missionaries from Iona, led by Aidan, selected as their base of work the island of Lindisfarne, where they built a monastery similar to that at Iona. The simple Irish monks succeeded within a generation in converting the mass of the English population and carried their work as far south as the Thames, where they joined forces with the Roman mission. Contact between the Celtic and Roman forms of Christianity brought into sharp focus their distinctive features of organization and discipline. Though the two groups were thoroughly in accord in doctrine, controversy developed in matters of religious practice, particularly their differing systems of computing the date of Easter. A conference held at the monastery of Whitby in 664 to settle points of dispute resulted in a decision favoring the Roman practice.

In 669 there arrived in Canterbury a remarkably able and learned Greek from Tarsus, named Theodore, who was sent by the pope to be archbishop. Theodore did more than anyone else to weld together the best elements of Celtic and Roman Christianity in England. The Irish admired Theodore's great learning, and Theodore in turn appreciated the unselfish devotion and intellectual capacities of the Irish. Wherever possible Theodore used the men trained in Celtic monastic discipline. But he thoroughly reorganized the English church in accord with the episcopal system established on the Continent, instituting bishops in dioceses of clearly defined boundaries and checking the Celtic tendency to wander about independent of ecclesiastical authority.

The glory of the English church in the time of Theodore and for a generation after his death (690) was its monasteries. They inherited the finest traditions of scholarship and religious zeal from both Celtic and Continental Christianity. Best known and justly famous among them were the twin monasteries of Wearmouth and Jarrow, whose founder and first abbot made five visits to Rome and the Continent to procure books, pictures, and other treasures for the churches and library of his establishment. His monks lived according to the Benedictine *Rule*. In this house lived and taught the Venerable Bede (d. 735) the greatest scholar of his time, to whom we are indebted for almost all our knowledge of Christianity in early England in his extraordinarily acute and reliable *Ecclesiastical History of the English Nation.*

The English and Irish monasteries exchanged students. Interestingly enough, it was an English monk named Egbert, living in Ireland, who gave impulse to a movement for the evangelization of the pagan Germans inhabiting the lands of the Rhine. To this new field of mission work numbers of English and Irish gave their lives. Chief among them was the Englishman Boniface (d. 754), who will be noticed in the next section. Through these valiant apostles, many of whom, like Boniface, suffered a martyr's fate, Christianity was firmly planted in Germany, and to the Continent were brought the high standards of learning and discipline of the church in the British Isles to serve as a leaven in the reform and advance of church life in western Europe.

CHAPTER III

CHRISTIANITY IN MEDIEVAL EUROPE

9. CHRISTIANITY IN THE CAROLINGIAN AGE

The recovery of order.—During the two centuries between Augustine and Gregory the Great western Europe had come under the sway of new peoples. Of these the Franks had already assumed the leadership. They had extinguished the Burgundian and reduced the Visigothic kingdom; they were yet, with the favor of the popes, to destroy the Lombard power in Italy. The Latin culture—the medium in which the Western church had arisen—was lost to all but a few book-lovers. Amid general barbarism thoughtful men saw the end of an era, and some of them supposed they were witnessing the closing scenes of history itself.

But the disordered world possessed the materials for reconstruction. The institutional framework of life for all classes was now to be provided by the hierarchical church and the Frankish state. It is true that the seventh century witnessed a halt in Frankish expansion while internal conflict raged. This strife was partly due to territorial sectionalism, partly to the insurgence of powerful landlords against a line of kings equally barbarous and incompetent. Soon after his savage execution of the wicked Brunhilda (613), Clothar II was forced to concede privileges to the church and the landed chieftains and to permit the separation of the Merovingian domain into three autonomous sections: Neustria in the western area, Burgundy in the south, and Austrasia in the east. Dagobert I (621–39) forced a temporary unification; but after him came a half-century of dissension and war. The "do-nothing kings" still nominally reigned, but those who ruled were their officers, the mayors of the palace.

Some measure of public decency was secured through the influence of two remarkable Austrasian leaders, Arnulf of Metz (d. 641) and Pippin of Landen (d. 640). Pippin was mayor in Austrasia; both were men of piety, character, and political talent. It is of historical importance that Arnulf's son Ansegisel married Pippin's daughter Begga (630); for by their marriage was founded the Arnulfing or Carolingian house. Pippin of Heristal, the child of this marriage, by a victory over the Neustrians in 687 brought to a close the long period of conflict and restored unity of administration. His death (714) was the signal for renewed strife; but his natural son Charles, called Martel (Hammer), soon mastered all Frankland. Charles defeated the Saracens who had overrun Spain and a great part of France. He also lent his favor to the missionaries who were seeking to convert to Christianity the pagan fringe on the east of the Frankish territories.

Religious leadership in the Frankish lands came in a remarkable degree from Ireland and England. Many of the earlier English missionaries, such as Willibrord, who with the favor of Pippin became archbishop of Utrecht (695), had been trained in Irish monasteries. The greatest missionary of the eighth century was Winfrith of Crediton in Devonshire, better known as St. Boniface (680–754). Authorized by the popes and protected by Charles Martel (714–42), Boniface gave organization to the existing German church and sowed Christianity among the tribes of Friesland, Hesse and parts of Thuringia. He was also the founder of monasteries that were to prove nurseries of the faith. As archbishop of Mainz (743) he was primate of Germany. Numerous other effective missionaries from England (both men and women) labored in Germany during the eighth century.

In the latter half of that century the co-operation of the church and the Frankish government reached its full significance. The succession of the House of Arnulf to that of Clovis was at last confirmed when, with the full consent of Pope Zachary, Pippin, miscalled the Short (742–68), son of Charles Martel, setting aside the last pitiable Merovingian, assumed the Frankish kingship (752). A religious anointing, at which Boniface may have officiated, accompanied his elevation. Three years later Pippin was reconsecrated by the pope himself. Pope Stephen III had come to the court at Ponthion urgently pleading for military aid against his aggressive Lombard neighbors. Soon afterward Pippin entered Italy, smote the Lombards, and gave the pope possession of the lands in Italy which they had snatched from the weakened Byzantine Empire. The Lombards continued, however, to menace the papacy until, urged by Pope Hadrian I, Charlemagne led a powerful army against them and extinguished their kingdom (774).

Charlemagne and the papacy.—In the long and glorious reign of Karl the Great (768–814), whom medieval romance writers and most modern historians have called Charlemagne, the co-operation of the papacy and the royal power was close and generally harmonious. The mutually advantageous alliance culminated in the imperial coronation of the gigantic Frank at Rome on Christmas Day, 800, by Pope Leo III, whom Charlemagne had delivered from his Roman enemies. It is not quite certain how this ceremony was planned, but we may hardly accept the statement of his biographer Einhard that Karl was taken by surprise in the pope's act. Nor can we be quite sure what ideas of papal-imperial relationships were in the minds of the participants in and the witnesses of this celebrated scene. It is certain, however, that under the influence of Alcuin, and of Augustine's *City of God*, Charlemagne was accustomed to think of himself as a theocratic ruler. He had previously written to offer Leo "an inviolable treaty of mutual fidelity," pledging his power to defend the faith in return for the intercession and benediction of the holy Roman church.

"In one of his letters to Leo," writes Douglas Woodruff (*Charlemagne* [Appleton-Century Co., 1935], p. 94), "Charles likens the Pope to Aaron and himself to Moses. It was a good image. Aaron might be the High Priest, but Moses led the chosen people of the Lord." His thought was to support and to co-operate with the pope, not to obey him. In some respects, notably in his rejection of the adoration of images, Charlemagne led the Frankish church to adopt positions out of accord with those taken at Rome. With the imperial crown Karl gained no territory and no material power. But the new formalities which he introduced at this court indicate that he felt himself advanced to a new dignity among princes.

Church reform.—The alliance was favorable to religion and culture, and the period consisting of the last half of the eighth and the first quarter of the ninth century was one of fresh vitality and hopeful achievement. Even within the reign of Pippin (742–68) the church of the Franks began to take on new life through the efforts of Boniface and the continuators of his work. One of the latter was Chrodegang, bishop of Metz (d. 766), a trusted friend of the king and his agent on a mission to Pope Stephen III. Chrodegang is best remembered for his partially successful effort to bring the clergy of his diocese under a common discipline for religion and study. He wrote a rule for the guidance of the houses of canons, as the priests living in these disciplined communities were called. Centuries earlier Augustine of Hippo had organized the clergy of his diocese in a somewhat similar way. But Chrodegang in his provisions for the worship and readings to be followed was partly under the influence of monastic practice. Other bishops introduced the plan; and fifty years after its author's death his rule, with some enlargements, was appointed for use throughout the empire. Of course, it was never possible to make it universal, especially in the case of priests in remote rural parishes, and clerical ignorance and irregularity of life still widely prevailed. In the ninth century the canons of Chrodegang gained institutional privileges and lost their sincerity.

The spirit of revival and reform is exhibited in many measures adopted under Charlemagne's government. The great monarch before and after his coronation as emperor appointed the bishops in his domain and assumed control of ecclesiastical affairs. It was his habit to hold spring and autumn assemblies of the nobles and clergy in order to obtain information from his dominions and to promulgate laws and regulations for government. Many of these meetings were concerned largely with church matters and may be regarded as ecclesiastical synods. The decisions taken were issued with the authority of the king; they offer abundant evidence of a sustained attempt to advance the character, learning, and religious efficiency of both priests and monks. Karl developed an earlier practice of sending royal visitors (*missi dominici*) in pairs consisting of a layman and a cleric to inspect and reform local institutions, adjudge disputes, and check the behavior of the clergy, monks, and nuns.

Educational reforms.—Charlemagne was eager to reform the monasteries and to promote good learning in them. As he wrote to Baugulf of Fulda in a letter intended for all prelates and abbots, monks were to be "devout and learned, chaste in life and correct in speech." Abbots and bishops were repeatedly exhorted to establish schools, to correct the service-books, and to multiply manuscripts in accurate transcriptions.

For the episcopal office Charlemagne selected the

most capable men. Renowned among his appointees is Theodulf, whom he made bishop of Orleans (d. 821). Theodulf wrote a versified treatise to reform the judiciary and a set of regulations for priests that was later widely circulated. He is to be commended, too, for a definite attempt to establish parish schools in which all children sent by their parents might be instructed free of charge.

Such provision for universal education was thoroughly in accord with Charlemagne's own ideas. But his promotion of education was hindered by the lack of learned men in his dominions, and he trusted largely to foreign scholars for leadership in the advance of learning. Few of those connected with the effort were Franks. Theodulf was of Visigothic origin. A number of scholars about the court were Irishmen. The historian Paul the Deacon, whose *Book of Homilies* was circulated by the government, was a Lombard. The great teacher Alcuin (d. 804), master of the Palace School, was an Englishman, trained in the school of York which inherited a fine tradition from Irish and English scholars. One of Alcuin's teachers was Egbert (archbishop of York, 732–66), who had been associated with the Venerable Bede.

The Palace School, reformed rather than created by Charlemagne and Alcuin, became an important center of education not only for the sons of princes and high nobles but for other talented youth. In this school, and in the monastery of Tours in which he spent his later years, Alcuin was the inspiring teacher of many men who came to distinction in the early ninth century. He was the author of numerous text-books, chiefly, in dialogue, as aids to the study of the liberal arts. This convenient division of learning into seven departments—grammar, rhetoric, and dialectic; arithmetic, geometry, music, and astronomy—de-rives from a work by a fifth-century Carthage Platon-ist, Martianus Capella. Boethius in the sixth century grouped the first three of these as the trivium and the other four as the quadrivium. The liberal arts were treated in innumerable textbooks in the Middle Ages, though most of these were based upon the works of Boethius and other early writers, including that most popular of all textbook writers, the fourth-century grammarian Donatus, a teacher of Jerome. These studies were also celebrated in poetry and depicted in art. Some of the writers both of the treatises and of the poems were pupils of Alcuin or of his associates in the Carolingian revival. Others were Irish scholars, num-bers of whom entered Charlemagne's empire, and some of whom attained to distinction in his service. Such were Clemens Scotus, who preceded Alcuin as head of the Palace School; Dungal, who was employed to reform a monastery in the former Lombard capital of Pavia; and Dicuil, who under Louis the Pious wrote a notable textbook of geography.

The early years of Louis (814–41) gave promise of a continuance of the Carolingian renaissance. Monastic schools with capable instructors flourished increasing-ly. But invasion from without and contention within the empire soon began to tell adversely upon church and school, and before the end of the century the ranks of the learned became thin indeed. Perhaps the most widely informed scholar of the whole era was Alcuin's favorite pupil, Rabanus Maurus (d. 856), who, as abbot of Fulda and later as archbishop of Mainz, in his teaching and writing labored to recover the knowledge of former ages and to promote monastic and clerical discipline and study. But the most original and brilliant mind was that of the Irishman, John Scotus Erigena (d. *ca.* 877), who somehow acquired a mastery of Greek, translated Greek mystical works into Latin, and wrote in a bold and luminous way of nature, reason, and God.

Alfred the Great.—Centuries later the story was told that Erigena spent his last years teaching in an English monastery. Certainly teachers were needed in England, where church and people had suffered greatly for two generations from the Danish invasions, and the knowledge of Latin was almost extinct. A new educational revival arose in the kingdom of Wessex under Alfred the Great (871–99), who, like Charlemagne, drew to his side numerous foreign scholars and promoted monastic learning. Since it was impossible immediately to impart to the priests and monks a reading knowledge of Latin, Alfred and his helpers translated for their instruction some of the great books of the past. But soon again in England the political basis of a progressive culture was shattered. The tenth century was a time of darkness and confusion throughout Europe. Only here and there a measure of security was afforded and the light of religion and of learning shone with promise for the future.

10. The Papacy as a World-Power

Weakness of kings and popes.—From the barbarized
fifth to the feudalized eleventh century, the need of
some integrating power was keenly felt in Europe.
Charlemagne came near to achieving a European
unity; but a century after him his empire was extinct.
In the person of Otto II the Saxon house of German
kings (919–1024) revived the imperial office (962); but
none of the Saxons, and none of the Franconians who
followed them (1024–1125), held Europe in their
sway as Charlemagne had done. The Capetian kings
of France (987–1328) were building the institutions
that would one day raise their power above that of
emperors, and the English Normans (1066–1154) and
Anjevins (1154–1272) were likewise free from the German power. It was in fact not so much kings or emperors as feudal barons who ruled the people. These
local magnates resisted all centralized authority and
kept society in a state of armed lawlessness.

Familiarity with the high claims and powers of
later and greater popes may lead us to forget how
modest was the role of the papacy in the earlier centuries of the Middle Ages, and how slow and halting
was its rise. Between Gregory the Great and Nicholas
I (858–67) most popes were fortunate to enjoy the co-
operation without demanding the obedience of rulers.
Within the ranks of the clergy the sense of obligation to
the pope was limited. The greater prelates, such as the
venerable Hinkmar of Rheims (d. 882), tried to con-
centrate church power in the provincial organization.

Nicholas I, indeed, asserted most of the later claims. But in the early tenth century the papacy was repeatedly bestowed upon the favorites of profligate adventuresses connected with the Roman aristocracy. The end of that century saw, in Sylvester II, new promise of reform. But again corrupt factions gained control. When three contenders for the office were locked in combat, the emperor Henry III, who made Charlemagne his model, marched into Italy, removed them all, had his own German nominee elected in Rome, and was crowned by him on Christmas Day, 1046.

Canon law and forged documents.—But the revival of the papacy was not to be directed by emperors. Many churchmen saw the need of the church's independence of secular rulers and resented Henry's well-meant but ominous interference. They opposed the existing secularization of the church and the appointment to clerical offices by feudality and kings, which had long been customary. They were students of the canon law, the accumulated decisions of popes and councils, which tended to enhance the papal claims. Moreover, these claims were supported by spurious documents compiled in the eighth and ninth centuries. According to the *Donation of Constantine* (*ca.* 774) that emperor had deeded to Pope Sylvester I and his successors "Italy and the regions of West" and affirmed the elevation of the pope above the emperor. Charlemagne's coronation came accordingly to be interpreted as the bestowal of the empire by the pope upon the prince of his choice—the "transfer of empire" from the ancient Roman to the German state. The *Forged Decretals* (*ca.*

850) asserted papal authority against the archbishops and ecclesiastical rights against secular power. To those who, desiring the deliverance of the church from its feudal entanglements, studied the genuine and spurious documents of canon law, a strengthened and reformed papacy seemed the only hope. In this spirit was devised the College of Cardinals (1059), a body whose function was to elect the popes, and whose members were appointed by previous popes. Thus was provided a means toward the independence and self-perpetuation of the papacy.

Hildebrand.—The dynamic little archdeacon Hildebrand was the leading advocate of reform at Rome in the sixties, and in 1073 he became Pope Gregory VII. His bold policy snatched for the papacy the initiative in world-affairs, and with intemperate zeal he pressed for reform of the teeming evils within the church. Reaffirming the provisions of canon law, he suspended the married clerics and forbade the laity to attend their services until they should dismiss their wives. This effort met with much resistance, and it can only be said that it initiated a long struggle to make clerical celibacy a reality.

Far more momentous was Hildebrand's attack upon the secular powers. Bishops had been appointed by the Frankish kings, and from the ninth century their installation was attended by the ceremony of royal investiture in which the king as suzerain conferred upon the bishop as vassal not only the insignia of secular office but the episcopal staff as well. This seemed the dramatization of an anomaly; the lay ruler seemed to claim by it spiritual superiority to the bishop. Such a claim indeed appeared to be implied in his appointment to the office, apart from investiture itself. Hildebrand attacked "lay investiture" and strove to make episcopal elections a church matter. From the side of the ruler this meant an intolerable loss of support from ecclesiastical vassals. The resulting conflict was intense and embittered. Hildebrand excommunicated the emperor Henry IV and released his subjects from their oaths of fealty. To gain time, Henry submitted at Canossa. He renewed the fight and carried it to Rome itself, but retired when Guiscard, master of the Normans in Italy, answered the pope's call for help. The Norman, however, ravaged the city and carried the pontiff to Salerno, where he died (1085). Hildebrand had stormy relations also with Philip I of France; and William the Conqueror, whom he regarded as the best of kings, refused to yield him fealty. By letters and legates he attempted to direct the policies of rulers in all Europe. He met with reverses and disappointments, but he had opened a campaign which under more prudent and patient leadership would largely achieve its object—papal supremacy and world-mastery.

Papacy against empire.—One of those who advanced the papal cause was the eloquent monk of Cluny who became Urban II (1088–99). He compelled Henry IV to leave Italy and launched the First Crusade (1095). The turbulent baronage that had disturbed the West was now to be drained off to a war of expansion in the East. The depletion of the nobles in war aided the cause of the royal power, thus checking in the end the added prestige which accrued to the papacy by its promotion of the Crusades.

In England a conflict over investiture between Archbishop Anselm and the Norman kings ended in an agreement whereby bishops were to be invested with ring and staff by the hierarchy but to do homage to the king for their estates (1107). Similar in principle was the Concordat of Worms (1122), between the emperor and the pope. But thus to recognize in procedure a distinction between a bishop's spiritual and feudal functions did not lighten the burden or remove the temptations of his secular tasks. Moreover, since the popes continued to affirm a universal suzerainty and to intervene in politics, fresh conflicts with princes were inevitable.

The brilliant, unhappy Hohenstaufen emperor, Frederick Barbarossa, engaged in a sanguinary struggle to extend the imperial power in Italy. Encouraged by the principles of Roman law, the study of which was then being revived at Bologna, Frederick tried to avoid any recognition of papal political superiority. The ceremony of holding the stirrup for a feudal superior was (in accordance with a story in the *Donation of Constantine*) performed by weak emperors for popes in 858 and in 1131. When Frederick met the English pope, Adrian IV, he first refused this esquire service but was induced grudgingly to perform it. The ceremony symbolized the Pope's suzerainty; but Barbarossa repudiated the theory that the empire was a papal fief. It was only after his long wars and defeat by the

Lombard cities that the proudest of emperors, kneeling on his own outspread cloak, kissed the feet of Pope Alexander III, and some days later held the pope's stirrup when he mounted, and led his horse (1177). In the same decade England saw the public penance of King Henry II for the murder of Becket, a prelate who had been the king's appointee but had fought for the church against the king.

Innocent III.—It was in the thirteenth century that the papacy attained to its greatest dignity and authority. The popes of that era, and their theological partisans, taught in exalted phrases the doctrine of a papal divine monarchy of the world. The able and learned Innocent III (1198–1216) applied to himself Jer. 1:10: the pope was "set over the nations and the kingdoms." The papacy was to the empire as the sun to the moon; the pope was the Vicar of Christ. The canon lawyers spoke of the pope's "fulness of power in things spiritual and in things temporal." Innocent formally awarded the empire to a Guelf prince who later opposed his policies and finally aided the young Hohenstaufen prince known to history as Frederick II, the Wonder of the World, to gain the throne. He fought a long battle with John of England over the appointment of an archbishop of Canterbury. John, deserted by his vassals, was forced to become a vassal of the pope. But Stephen Langton, the archbishop of Innocent's choice, led the English barons in compelling the king to sign Magna Charta (1215), which the pope vehemently denounced. Philip II of France, attracted by the charms and talents of Agnes of Meran, dismissed his

Danish wife, Ingeborga, and refused to submit to the pope's demand that he restore the injured queen.

In his conflicts with John and Philip, Innocent made effective use of the spiritual weapons of excommunication and interdict. The interdict deprived of the services of the church, including the sacrament of marriage and burial in consecrated ground, all persons within a designated area. It often succeeded in causing such public distress that recalcitrant rulers were obliged to come to terms. Not only in the cases mentioned but in more than fifty other instances, Innocent employed the interdict to obtain his ends; in some cases the threat of it was enough. But in France and elsewhere the papal interdict awakened resentment as well as terror; and it gradually ceased to be an effective weapon in politics. Innocent cautiously permitted the rise of the friar orders. He set afoot a vigorous war against heretics in southern France. After denouncing the Fourth Crusade he accepted its results which for a time extended the Latin church over the Greek Empire. The council which he held in 1215 enacted extensive reforms.

Successors of Innocent.—Innocent III and his successors, Honorius III, Gregory IX, and Innocent IV (d. 1254), exercised authority over the nations great and small, but not without much resistance and many bitter conflicts involving grave crises for the papacy. Frederick II (1214–50) proved the most consistently antipapal of all the emperors. He long refused to go on crusade as he had promised, and, when he did go, he was under excommunication. He procured with ease the mastery of Jerusalem and placed the crown of that crusaders' kingdom upon his own head. Even King Louis IX of France, famed as saint and crusader, had his disagreements with Innocent IV; and the hostility of the English and French nobles and kings during this pontificate to the methods of papal taxation offer a forecast of later strife of popes and nations. Opposition to the abuses connected with papal appointments became intense at times, and in this matter Robert Grosseteste (d. 1253), the scholarly bishop of Lincoln, offered vigorous resistance to the pope. Gregory X (1271–76) was the last pope who attained any large measure of success in his political policy. When at the end of the century Boniface VIII (1294–1303) engaged in a struggle with Philip IV of France, he met with humiliation and defeat.

Decline of the papacy.—Under French influence the papacy took up its residence at Avignon on the Rhone (1309–77), and the popes, to maintain their revenues, invented new and burdensome taxes. The "captivity" at Avignon was followed by the schism in which one papal claimant resided at Rome, the other at Avignon. Corruption and confusion prevailed. Men sought reunion and reform by general councils of the church, and the schism was virtually ended by the Council of Constance (1414–18). The councils, as representing the whole body of Christians, declared their authority to be superior to that of the popes. This doctrine of representative government by means of elective councils is known as conciliarism. But the new line of popes that followed in the fifteenth century repudiated conciliarism and revived a policy of centralization. While they still asserted a supernational authority, they negotiated concordats with the nations instead of commanding them. The Renaissance era brought a fresh flood of scandalous evils in papal administration, and the lives of some of the popes were notoriously wicked. With popes like Alexander VI (1492–1503) and Julius II (1503–13) on the throne the political power of the office rested largely on its Italian possessions and on its success in the competition of diplomacy, intrigue, and war in which it engaged with other states of Italy.

11. Religious Life in the Middle Ages

Ascetic religion.—In the Middle Ages when people spoke of "religion" they implied some sort of ascetic discipline, and monks and friars were specially known as the "religious." The story of the early Christian ascetic movement and of the rise of monasticism has been briefly told in chapter ii. It will be remembered that about the time of Benedict of Nursia the monastic life of Ireland was flourishing and beginning to expand. Famous among a hundred well-known Irish monks abroad was Columbanus (d. 615), who labored in Gaul and Italy. These missionary monks established numerous monasteries of the Irish type, marked by severe asceticism and intellectual vigor. Their services to Continental Christianity were highly important. But in course of time Benedictine monasticism, with its better organization and more moderate ascetic demands, came to prevail.

Benedict of Aniane.—We noted above Charlemagne's efforts on behalf of education in the monasteries of his empire. Besides this government pressure for reform there is to be noted the spontaneous revival of monastic devotion led by Benedict of Aniane. Witiza, the Visigothic soldier, became Benedict the monk, and finding his brethren ill disciplined, formed his own intensely ascetic group at Aniane in Languedoc (779). The group grew into a populous community, and Benedict became associated with Alcuin and an influential leader in the church. Louis the Pious as administrator of Aquitaine admired his work, and, when Louis succeeded Charlemagne in 814, he induced Benedict to establish a monastery near Aachen. The rule which Benedict of Aniane adopted was based upon that of Benedict of Nursia, but it owed something to the author's study of numerous other monastic documents. Benedict was appointed general inspector of the monasteries of the empire, and his rule was authorized for general adoption (817). But the aged "abbot of abbots" died (821) before the reform could become far-reaching.

The Cluny reform.—The next important revival was that which centered at Cluny in what was then Burgundy. It was founded in the troublous early tenth century (910) in the days of one of the most despicable of the popes of that era of depravity. For two centuries Cluny and the hundreds of monasteries which it reformed and attached to its system offered a home for sincere religion and made the influence of the ascetic ideal felt increasingly in the church. A series of able and earnest abbots of Cluny, from Odo (d. 942) to Hugh the Great (d. 1109), built the Cluny connection as a highly centralized and efficient organization. Hugh ruled Cluny for sixty-one years and was an adviser of kings and popes. Under him the Cluniacs gave valuable support to the papal reforms. Never extreme in asceticism, they became relaxed after the death of Hugh, and, although discipline was restored by Peter the Venerable (d. 1156), the congregation of Cluny no longer attracted the most devout spirits.

Many other new starts in monasticism had already been made. The movements under Gerard de Brogne (d. 959) in the Netherlands and under Dunstan (d. 988) and others in England had no little importance. A tenth-century movement in Calabria and later Italian movements, such as the Camaldolensians (1012) and the Vallambrosans (1038), show a fresh influence from Eastern monasticism. The revivals north of the Alps remained essentially Benedictine, though with wide variations. Noteworthy among these is that which produced the Carthusian order (1084). It was founded by the able Bruno of Cologne on the strictest ascetic principles. Like most other strict groups, it remained relatively small.

The Cistercians.—The new movement which outrivaled Cluny was the Cistercian order, founded by a migration of discontented aspirants to monastic holiness from an ill-disciplined house. They settled in the forest wilderness of Cîteaux (1098), thirty miles north of Cluny, and, living in great poverty under their abbot Stephen Harding of Sherborne, began to attract recruits. From Cîteaux other new monasteries began to be founded. Harding produced, and the monks adopted, a remarkable constitution which, in contrast to that of the Cluniacs, involved a system of representative government. Cîteaux, too, consciously diverged from Cluny at other points. Taking seriously Benedict's teaching on industry, the monks spent less time in worship and more in work. At first they engaged in the heavy labor necessary to their survival in the wilderness places where they chose for ascetic reasons to plant their colonies. This led to great operations of land-clearing and agriculture in which they employed lay help. They kept on for a century planting numerous houses, clearing and draining land, and raising cattle, horses, sheep, and poultry. Their economic contribution to Europe began to eclipse their spiritual influence, and, while they did not become grossly corrupt, they became deeply involved in worldly matters.

The most renowned of Cistercians was Bernard (d. 1153), who at twenty-two presented himself at Cîteaux with a company of recruits from feudalism to monasticism, became the first abbot of Clairvaux, was everywhere famous as the opponent of heretics, ardently preached the Third Crusade, and by his mystical writings made a deep and lasting impression.

The cloister stood over against the castle in the feudal world. It afforded to ascetic piety a retreat from military brutality. The leadership of monasticism was drawn from the aristocracy, and many a scarred warrior took refuge within monastic walls to spend his last days in penance for his misdeeds. All the great monastic movements also provided numerous houses for women; and when unmarried women had no function in society at large, in the nunneries they found protection and opportunity for mutual service and edification. A few of them became distinguished for mystical or intellectual attainment. It was in monasteries, too, that the literary classics of antiquity were transmitted to later ages. Their active attention to secular education was significant but limited. For essentially the monk was one who was concerned for the salvation of his own soul. To form any contact with the outer world was in some degree a violation of his principles. It was despite its intention that monasticism became economically and socially important.

The friar movements.—As the monastic movements reacted to feudalism, so did the friar orders react to the new town conditions. Unlike the monks the friars began as active religious leaders of the people. Francis of Assisi (d. 1226) was the son of a merchant. He revolted from his father's business ways, identified himself with the poor, and undertook the service of "Lady Poverty" (1209). He was fascinated by the poverty and sufferings of Christ; but, unlike the heretics who preached apostolic poverty, he was sincerely loyal to the church and the priesthood. His movement was socially directed from the first. It carried to the townsfolk a message of repentance, peace, and brotherliness. Later the Franciscans broke into two great sections—one rigorous, the other compromising—on the doctrine of poverty; and groups of the rigorous or "spiritual" Franciscans came to be regarded as heretical and were ruthlessly persecuted. All in all, Francis did much to set in motion radical forces in Western society.

The founder of the Dominicans, Dominic of Osma (d. 1221), was also concerned largely with the urban classes. His work began amid the Albigenses, heretics of southern France who had privileges under the count of Toulouse. His group grew about him as propagandists of orthodoxy, and his order, the Preaching Friars, produced many able theologians and manned the papal Inquisition against heretics.

In the later Middle Ages came a general decline of ascetic religion. In the more stable and better-educated society some of the functions of monasticism were otherwise provided. The common man lost his reverence for the cloister, and recruits were fewer and less desirable persons than formerly. Many monks were religiously languid and many monasteries highly corrupt. The friar orders shared in this decadence though not to the same degree. New groups arose, like the Brethren of the Common Life (1378), which aimed to combine the contemplative with the active life. But in part through the stirring sermons of the friars, in part through the activities of biblical heretics like the Waldenses and the Lollards, and in part through the growth of intelligence in the towns, religion was becoming more a matter of the lay people.

Religion in lay life.—In the early Middle Ages the religion of the layman was a combination of ancestral pagan superstition and of such church guidance and teaching as he might be fortunate enough to receive.

Fragments of pagan ritual and a variety of forms of magic and divination entered intimately into daily life. Often forbidden by the church, these practices were never eradicated. In the late Middle Ages there was a fresh revival of witchcraft, and all the dark beliefs and cruelties of the witch mania were in full vogue. The cult of saints and relics was very attractive to the medieval man, and saints' days gave relief from work for piety or pleasure. Lives of the saints were read aloud; these related abundant miracles which fed the imagination and heroic sacrifices that stimulated piety. But more and more laymen were becoming intelligent about their religion. There was a great increase of preaching, which was sometimes sensational and sometimes instructive. Peter Waldo (*ca.* 1173), John Wyclif (d. 1384), and John Huss (d. 1415) founded movements which industriously spread the vernacular Scriptures. Other writers prepared simple books for lay reading, explaining, often with illustrative stories, the Creed, the Lord's Prayer, the Commandments, the seven virtues, the seven sins, the seven sacraments, the seven works of mercy spiritual and physical—a body of teaching easily learned and practical for daily living. The layman, too, was acquiring some ability to criticize and was often incredulous of the claims of the clergy. Although there was little to rival the church as a center of social life, many attended church only rarely. Thus the late medieval scene shows superstition, credulity, intelligent piety, and sheer irreligion among the lay folk of the towns, with a manifest tendency away from clerical control.

12. MEDIEVAL AND RENAISSANCE CULTURE AND LEARNING

Retarded progress of education.—From the ninth to the twelfth century education made little progress. It lacked institutional stability and failed to make a persistent assault upon the ignorance of the times. When the learned men were celibates, the home was not likely to become the nursery of learning. Monastic schools there were; they achieved something, but little of permanent significance in the diffusion of education. Under Louis the Pious they were prohibited from teaching those not in or preparing for monastic life, but little attention was paid to this rule. A fair number of monasteries we know held more or less efficient schools for the children of their neighborhoods. In perhaps a score of houses learning was intensely cultivated, but rarely for more than two generations in succession. Similarly varying fortunes mark the life of the episcopal or cathedral schools, which in the late tenth century began to surpass those of the cloisters. Through the eleventh century the curriculum was still, for both sorts of schools, a partial or complete program of the seven liberal arts.

The twelfth century saw a revival of the intellectual and cultural life. In numerous instances the cathedral schools took on fresh vitality, and chiefly in two ways: they increasingly became centers for the expansion of education and their teachers were interested in new questions. Grammar schools and song schools, supported and directed by the church or by the rising town guilds, and vernacular and technical schools as well, now multiplied and spread their influence. Still more fruitful was the work of a few wandering research scholars. These intellectual explorers, such as Adelard of Bath, Raymond of Toledo, Gerrard of Cremona, Michael Scot, and Herman the German, formed contacts with Jewish and Arab scholars in Sicily and Spain and, between 1100 and 1250, presented Latin translations of a vast number of treatises on philosophy and science, including the physical and metaphysical works of Aristotle. Crusaders might overrun Moslem lands; but the scholars of the church had now to wrestle not only with the giants of Moslem thought but with the mighty Aristotle himself, "the master," as Dante said, "of those who know." The Western mind awoke to the labor and strife of the scholastic era.

The universities.—In the same era came the beginnings of universities. A variety of circumstances attended their origins. At Salerno the mineral springs brought health seekers and their physicians, and the university gathered about a medical school. At Bologna all was subordinated to the study of law. There Irnerius (d. 1130) and many after him expounded Justinian's code, and the students organized a guild or corporation for which the common name was *universitas*. At Paris students congregated to hear Abailard (d. 1142), that incomparable lecturer and debater, assail the realism of William of Champeaux. There it was the teachers, contentious though they were, who combined, about 1200, to form the corporation. Theology was the chief study at Paris; with it went logic and philosophy and the whole range of medieval knowledge. Similar was the emphasis at Oxford, where the fame of Robert Pulleyn (d. 1150) attracted students, and the later growth was partly by migration from Paris. But whatever the specialties emphasized in the universities, each of them added theology, law, and medicine to the now expanding studies of the trivium and quadrivium.

Aristotle and scholasticism.—Thus the thirteenth century began with Aristotle and the universities. At first some of the clergy tried to keep them apart, and the higher works of Aristotle were banned at Paris in 1210. It was largely owing to the labors of Dominican scholars, among whom the most distinguished were Albertus Magnus (d. 1280) and his greater pupil Thomas Aquinas (d. 1274), that Western Christians came to adopt the Aristotelian philosophy and use it to undergird the traditional dogma to which at first it seemed so alien.

Scholastic discussion of the time of Anselm (d. 1109) had been concerned with the question whether universal ideas have real existence. Anselm, a Platonic realist, answered "Yes" to this question; Roscellin, the nominalist, answered "No." Anselm saw the wood, Roscellin the trees. Applied, for example, to the doctrine of the Trinity, nominalism seemed a destructive heresy. As such it was condemned (1092). But Platonic realism, too, failed to guard orthodoxy. Aquinas wrought from Aristotle a view that has been called Aristotelian realism. The universal exists, but it exists in the individual thing. This was helpful toward establishing an ordered world of thought, relating God and phenomena, ideas and things. He took from Aristotle, too, the materials of his cosmological argument for the existence of God—the first mover of the universe in motion. The "Angelic Doctor" makes the end of life to consist in that felicity which is the contemplation of truth, ultimately, in the life to come, the contemplation of God. To that end all politics and economics and art are subordinate. Since the priesthood leads to that higher felicity, and secular governments have lower ends, the pope and the hierarchy are held to be above all earthly potentates. He expounds and defends the sacraments and discipline of the church, the doctrines of transubstantiation, penance and purgatory, and the punishment of heretics. Thus, as philosopher and theologian, Aquinas is a strong pillar of the papal church. His whole position was comforting to the church in its effort to build up a papal theocratic system. The great Dominican has acquired fresh authority in modern Roman Catholicism and is a vital force in the world today.

Franciscan scholastics.—The arguments of Aquinas were challenged at certain points by a school of Oxford Franciscans, of which Bishop Robert Grosseteste was the inspirer and Roger Bacon (d. 1264), advocate of experimental science, the most famous member. Some Dominicans, too, were his opponents.

Scholasticism passed through new stages under the English Franciscan influence in the early fourteenth century, and at Paris first Duns Scotus (d. 1308) and then William of Ockham (d. 1349?) gained many adherents. Ockham revived nominalism and so separated reason from faith that, while in some minds his thought bred skepticism, he had a part in stimulating both the Reformation, with its emphasis on faith, and the empiricism and rationalism of later philosophy. But the intellectual interests of his century were more in politics than in theology, and in its later half men's minds were coming under the spell of the Renaissance.

The Renaissance.—The Renaissance was a many-sided movement and marks a new era of individual expression in literature, art, science, and discovery. It arose in Italy, where favorable economic conditions and the rule of intellectually tolerant despots made possible the patronage of free scholars intent upon their own independent pursuits. It did not appear first in the universities, and, when it entered them, it lost vitality in their routine. Its first great prophet was Francesco Petrarca (Petrarch, d. 1374), who was sent in youth by his father to study law at Bologna. There is a story that his father found him ardently reading not the law but the Latin classics and in anger burned his books, rescuing Vergil and Cicero from the fire only in response to the boy's tears. Young Petrarch was to give much of his energy to the task of rescuing the classics not from fire but from mold. A new zeal for classical literature seized the ablest scholars of the time. Latin authors were read not as a means to the use of Latin in the traditional studies but for literary enjoyment and knowledge of the past. Pagan Aristotle had been put to Christian use by the scholastics, but many of the humanists were satisfied with the

pagans as they were. Petrarch admired Scipio Afri-
canus more than the Christian saints. After him came
a score of pioneers on the study of Greek, who employed imported teachers or visited Constantinople or
Athens to learn the language and literature of ancient
Greece. An intense devotion to these studies produced in men of genius literary results of the greatest
importance.

This new generation held in contempt the sterile
refinements of scholasticism. They were humanists,
men devoted to "humaner letters." But they were
humanists also in a larger sense. They were joyously
convinced of the worth-whileness of the study of man,
his mind, body, and estate, regardless of the doctrinal
framework in which man had been viewed by their
predecessors. They took off the colored glasses of medieval symbolism and looked about them with the
naked eye. Their favorite ethical idea was *virtù*, which
meant for them self-realization, and might easily be
perverted to authorize antisocial behavior. They were
largely self-trained and possessed exaggerated notions
of their own scholarship. Some were personally vain
and quarrelsome fellows, like Poggio and Filelfo,
whose literary exchanges in Florence set a record for
vituperation. But this should not blind us to the great
body of serious work achieved by the humanists which
not only revealed the culture of the ancients but made
literary languages of the vernaculars and permanently
altered men's thoughts of humanity itself.

Some Renaissance men, of whom Leonardo da Vinci
is best known, possessed scientific imagination; but

their experiments led not so much to the solution of great problems as to inventions, among which the printing press was of prime importance and numerous military devices had a place. But in due time came Copernicus (d. 1543), who left a new astronomy which it took scientists three-quarters of a century to adopt. The real scientific Renaissance came only in the seventeenth century. As yet science gave religion little to worry about.

The humanists and religion.—Most humanists (the negative Aristotelian Pomponazzi [d. 1525] is an exception), though despising the "cobwebs" of scholasticism, formerly adhered to the traditional dogmas. But at Florence Ficino (d. 1499) revived Plato under the influence of Neo-Platonism and sought a simplification of doctrine. His associate, John Pico della Mirandola, a more cautious Platonist, was the inspirer of Thomas More (d. 1535) in England. Plato, not Aristotle, was the ancient philosopher of the humanists, although Aristotle too was studied, and now with attention to the Greek text. A few Italian scholars, such as Gianozzo Manetti (d. 1459), gave critical attention to Hebrew. Lorenzo Valla (d. 1457), the greatest literary critic of the age, exposed by language study the fraudulence of the *Donation of Constantine* and rejected the apostolic origin of the Apostles' Creed.

But it was chiefly in the northern countries that Christian humanists engaged in a reverent criticism of the biblical texts. The use of the Greek Scriptures was not begun by Erasmus. John Colet (d. 1519), an Oxford scholar, one of the numerous Englishmen who since Chaucer's day had studied in Italy, in lectures on Paul revealed the possibilities of such an effort. A number of Dutch scholars connected with the Brethren of the Common Life learned to use Greek in their scriptural studies. But the work of Desiderius Erasmus (d. 1536) as editor of the Greek New Testament (1516) crowns the contribution of humanism to Christianity. At the same time Jacques Lefèvre (d. 1536) was engaged at Paris on New Testament and early church studies, and Cardinal Francisco Ximenez (d. 1517), the leader of a rigorous reform movement in Spain, produced another Greek edition of the New Testament, prepared before, but published after, that of Erasmus.

Renaissance art.—The contrast of medieval and Renaissance ideals is seen most vividly in the history of art. The anonymous architects and artists who left the lofty Gothic structures and interiors rich with saints and shrines to the admiration of all who are sensitive to spiritual beauty were succeeded by renowned individuals of genius who built to satisfy the craving for outward splendor or admiringly depicted the human face and form. The beauty of holiness and symbol gave place to the beauty of nudity and nature or to the colorful bravery of splendid robes proudly worn. Filippo Brunelleschi (d. 1446), with his spacious colonnades and daring dome, and Leon Alberti (d. 1472), learning from a book of Vitruvius, rediscovered by Poggio, the structure of the arch of Augustus and employing its principle in the façade of a church in Florence, may remind us how architecture responded to the new interests. Amid the flowering of Renaissance painting we may think of the naturalism of an amused young angel standing beside a madonna of Fra Lippo Lippi, Bellini's very human "Madonna of the Trees," Michelangelo's "Adam" and "Moses," the highly individualized apostles in Leonardo da Vinci's "Last Supper," the rich costume and handsome face of Titian's "Man in the Red Cap," and Holbein's completely satisfying portrait of Erasmus writing which is in itself a matchless reminder of humanism at work with brain and pen. The same impression is made through sculpture in Donatello's "David" and Cellini's "Perseus." It is that of a revolutionary enthusiasm for the human.

The pagan and secular trends of the Renaissance offered the gravest challenge to the church; but the record of the popes of the era shows how sadly the church failed to respond to the challenge until deterioration had reached a stage too critical for peaceful reform.

CHAPTER IV

CHRISTIANITY IN THE REFOR-
MATION ERA

13. LUTHER AND THE RISE OF PROTESTANTISM

Background of the Reformation.—Amid the changing conditions of sixteenth-century Europe Christianity took on new forms and new vigor. Grave controversies attended this revival, but it swept away much corruption and pretense and brought to light principles which men embraced with sincerity. It gave rise to Protestantism in its Lutheran and Reformed branches and to a series of left-wing groups; it profoundly altered the character of the Church of England; and it involved the reform of that part of the church which still clung to the papacy. Its Protestant aspect we call the Reformation; the papal reform is known as the Counter Reformation. Other terms, such as "Protestant Revolt," and "Catholic Revival," are employed by some historians.

Drastic religious changes were vaguely foretold by some anxious observers of conditions before Luther, but nobody could predict where the new forces would first appear. Germany, however, offered the natural stage for the drama. The German Empire was not, like France or England, a consolidated national state but a loose federation of small states; and it was initially more probable there than elsewhere that a daring reformer would find a local protector while his message gained acceptance. Such a protector Luther found in Frederick the Wise, elector of Saxony, a respected and influential prince.

Three other factors in the contemporary situation should be especially noted for their relation to the Reformation and its success: (1) humanism had produced its chief fruits and would henceforth be of less importance; (2) many nations had reached a stage of self-realization in which they would be unlikely to join any general action to preserve the papacy; and (3) a new sea commerce had arisen, which was attended by capitalistic development and the growth of monopolies and of money power. German companies were prominent in this new business world, and nowhere was the old economic order more painfully disturbed than in Germany. New burdens fell upon peasants and the poorer townsfolk. Only the great merchants prospered. Amid widespread distress and discontent burdensome church taxation called forth more resentment than it would otherwise have done.

Martin Luther.—There would have been a Reformation, but a very different one from that which happened, without Martin Luther (1483–1546), its German leader. His father struggled from the status of a free peasant to that of a fairly prosperous citizen of a small town in Saxony. Martin went to school at Magdeburg and Eisenach and to Erfurt University. Having taken a Master's degree, instead of studying law as his father wished, he entered an Augustinian monastery (1505). He became a priest and later a professor, first of philosophy and then of theology, at Wittenberg. As monk and teacher he entered deeply into the problems of religion and studied the Bible, together with some mystical works. He endured a period of grave personal conflict which modern psychology may help us to interpret. An introspective habit of mind and the clash of opposing ideas of salvation in his thinking gave intensity to the struggle. All his efforts to find comfort in the ascetic works of the cloister left him uncertain of God's favor. The Bible expression "justice (or righteousness) of God" became, as he said, "a thunderbolt in my conscience." He had thought of it as an unattainable standard by which he would be judged. But the phrase, "the just shall live by faith" (Rom. 1:17), shed on the problem a new light. Of this experience he wrote: "The passage became to me the true gate of Paradise." Faith, not works, was now for him the condition of justification before God, and faith was itself the gift of a gracious God. Thus arose his doctrine of "justification by faith"—a doctrine adverse to the prevailing scholastic conceptions of the value of good works. Luther went on for some years clarifying his new theology without attracting much notice.

Luther in controversy.—One of the practices supported by scholasticism was that of granting on prescribed conditions indulgences or authoritative pardons for sins that otherwise subjected the offender to acts of penance. At this period the selling of indulgences had become one of the most scandalous of abuses. Tetzel, a Dominican friar, was hawking indulgences in Ger-

many in a peculiarly objectionable way. Luther challenged his methods and his message in sermons and in
a series of ninety-five theses which he posted on the
door of the castle church at Wittenberg on Halloween,
1517—and the fat was in the fire.

A pamphlet controversy followed. Pope Leo X
(1513–21), son of Lorenzo de Medici, at first thought
of it as a quarrel of Dominicans and Augustinians.
Luther won so many adherents that the situation in
Germany became serious for the papacy. In a debate
with John Eck, an Ingoldstat professor, he was led to
admit that John Huss had been unjustly condemned.
His expulsion from the papal church now seemed a
probability. In his *Liberty of a Christian Man* he set
forth his religious message of justification and the
priesthood of all believers. By the latter he meant not
so much that every Christian is his own priest as that
Christians are priests to one another, "praying for
others and serving one another" in their daily work
and intercourse. He constantly emphasized the mutual and social character of Christianity. He also wrote
an appeal to those in authority to summon councils
for the reform of the church and repeatedly asked for a
general council to settle the issues raised, asserting in
the language of the earlier conciliarists the supremacy
of councils over popes.

The decade of the 1520's was crowded with events.
The young Charles I of Spain became Emperor
Charles V in 1520 and met his first diet at Worms in
1521. Frederick the Wise made it possible for Luther,
though he had been excommunicated, to be heard at

the diet, and the monk spoke his mind boldly and persuasively. Afterward in Frederick's castle of the Wartburg he worked on a German translation of the New Testament. Back in Wittenberg he encountered and overcame a radical movement led by "prophets" from Zwickau who claimed special revelations, and he drove out his former associate Carlstadt, who had come under their influence.

The knights in Germany rose in revolt (1522–23) aided by the humanist Ulrich von Hutten, who, in a spirit of patriotism, had hotly supported Luther. Luther opposed all armed rebellions, and a number of princes combined to crush the movement. Next the distressed peasants, joined by artisans of the towns, spread revolt and destruction over a large area of southern Germany (1524–25). Luther had warned their masters against oppression of the serfs, but, loathing revolt as the devil's work, he denounced destruction upon all engaged in it in the most unmeasured terms. Their forces were crushed and mercilessly destroyed by an army of the princes and cities. Luther was also engaged in a violent controversy with Erasmus, who had been moderately favorable to his movement, but was alienated by the fear that it would produce violence rather than reform and repelled by Luther's absolute predestinarianism. In these crises Luther, who had been hailed as a hero by many in all classes, lost support among knights, humanists, and common people but gained the permanent adherence of many princes and town governments.

Rise of Lutheranism.—Meanwhile, with the aid of

Philip Melanchthon and others, Luther finished his New Testament and in course of years published a German version of the Old Testament as well. The Luther Bible proved an important agency in promoting and giving character to the Reformation. Luther also put into the vernacular portions of the worship and after some years of its use published his *German Mass* and other liturgical works. Congregational worship was given new reality by the use of the spoken language and of a newly created body of German hymnody which grew up in the ensuing decades. Melanchthon published a simple exposition of the new doctrines; and statements of the faith made by Lutherans in various crises led to the important Confession of Augsburg, which was prepared by Melanchthon for the Diet of Augsburg of 1530, and which remained authoritative in Lutheran churches. Thus the rising Lutheran church was provided with the Bible and forms of worship in the vernacular and with a standard of belief.

The emperor wished to destroy Luther, but troubles elsewhere led him to spend the years 1521–29 outside Germany, unable to control German affairs. After a diet favorable to Luther in 1524, a papal legate organized a small league of princes to resist Lutheranism. This was later reorganized as the League of Dessau (1525) and was soon confronted by the League of Torgau (1526). Thus Germany was politically more than ever divided. The Diet of Speyer (1526) resolved that until the emperor's promise to obtain a general church council should be fulfilled each ruler should determine the religion of his own state. Already numerous free cities had adopted Lutheran reforms; as also had Prussia, then a small East Baltic state outside the empire, where the ruler and the leading bishops came under Luther's influence. Elsewhere in Germany most of the bishops were hostile to the Reformation, but the parish priests, except those rejected as unfit, generally, with varying degrees of reluctance or enthusiasm, accepted the change where it was introduced.

The decision of the diet of 1526 cleared the way for the Lutheranizing of states and cities. A visitation or inspection of the parishes in Electoral Saxony was followed by the organization of consistories which took over the government of the church. These consisted of laymen and clerics and were appointed by the state. A like development took place in Hesse, Brandenburg, Anhalt, and other states. Luther vaguely hoped for freedom of the church from the state, but thought this not yet practicable, and the powerful princes gained an unwholesome control of ecclesiastical affairs. Another diet met at Speyer in 1529. The emperor was now victorious in Italy and determined to act against Luther, and the majority of the diet favored such action. A minority stoutly protested on the ground that the oft-promised council had not been called and that, until it met, the unanimous decision of 1526 should be followed. For themselves they proposed to follow their consciences, which meant to retain Lutheranism —and the church lands which they had appropriated. While they asserted a doctrine of private judgment, they had no thought of permitting their subjects free choice of religion; but they probably genuinely desired a council which they hoped would produce peaceful settlement and reform. From their *Protest* comes the use of the word "Protestant." Later that year Luther met the Swiss reformer Huldreich Zwingli at Marburg. They were brought together to confer on the possibility of a common Protestant front; but, while they agreed on most of the points in discussion, Luther was hostile to Zwingli's view of the Lord's Supper, and, with Melanchthon, disinclined to form a political union with the Swiss. He still hoped for common reform action within the empire.

Expansion and defense of Lutheranism.—The Augsburg Confession set forth the Lutheran doctrines in moderate form but proved quite unsatisfying to the emperor, who had returned to Germany intent upon destroying Lutheranism. The Protestant princes were now given six months in which to abandon their Lutheran faith and reform policy. During this period (1531) they organized the League of Schmalkald and prepared to defend themselves against an expected attack by the emperor and such princes as would support him. War was delayed, however, by the necessity of a common defense against the Turks, who were now, under Suleiman the Magnificent, menacing the empire. Charles now sought a church council, believing that he could dominate it and so gain control of the churches of Germany. But Pope Clement VII strongly opposed a council, and Francis I of France, the emperor's enemy, sided with the pope against him and at the same time allied himself with Suleiman. By 1540 the Schmalkald League had added a number of states to its membership. In that year Philip of Hesse disgraced the Protestant cause by a bigamous marriage, and the League lost prestige. But Charles still felt it necessary to delay his intended war on the League, and soon afterward three conferences were held between Lutheran and Roman Catholic theologians in a vain effort to reach agreement.

In course of the thirties the kings of France and England sought the favor of the Lutherans with a view to weakening the emperor. Francis I invited Melanchthon and Bucer of Strassburg to consult on the reconstruction of the French church, but the opposition of the theologians and lawyers of Paris wrecked his plan. Henry VIII, entering upon a course of reform in England, sought connection with the Schmalkald League and invited Melanchthon to England; but his prince refused to let him go, and those who went, though encouraged by Archbishop Cranmer, soon found that Henry's policy had changed.

Martin Bucer (1491–1551), the reformer of Strassburg, was a Lutheran who had great influence in southern Germany but differed from Luther on the doctrine of the Eucharist and desired union with the Swiss Protestants. In 1530 he wrote the *Confession of of the Four Cities* for the Augsburg diet, but it was summarily rejected. He negotiated with Melanchthon and induced Luther to accept the Wittenberg Concord (1536), by which Lutheranism in Germany was unified. He was active in many efforts to bring together

Swiss and German Protestantism and ended his days in England in association with Cranmer. His influence was strongly felt also by John Calvin and other leaders of the Reformed church.

While Lutheranism was being consolidated in a great part of Germany, Luther's great career came to an end (1546). He had been married in 1525 to Katherine von Bora, a former nun, and had lived a happy family life, while preaching, teaching, and writing with great activity. His *Table Talk*, jotted down roughly by students who lived in his house, is a priceless record of his shrewd and humorous sayings.

After Luther's death Charles found an ally in Maurice of ducal Saxony, a traitor to the Schmalkalders, who, however, afterward opposed him. Two wars were fought to an inconclusive result, and the issues were settled in the Peace of Augsburg (1555). This peace left Germany divided into Lutheran and Roman Catholic states; but it was not seriously disturbed until the Thirty Years' War began (1618).

Lutheranism spread to Sweden, Denmark, and Norway and became in these kingdoms the established religion. The movement in Scandinavia involved the assertion of Swedish independence from Denmark, under Gustavus Vasa, and the subjection of Norway to Denmark. Bishops were retained in the churches of these nations, but all adopted the Augsburg Confession and the use of Scriptures and worship in the speech of the people.

Great changes in education attended the Lutheran Reformation, and these were largely guided by Me-

lanchthon and the Pomeranian reformer John Bugen-
hagen. Schools were created and universities were
extensively reformed. In the curricula of theology the
Bible was closely studied, with the Greek learning of
the Renaissance but not in its spirit. In the third
quarter of the century numerous minor theological
controversies were waged, but for Lutheranism these
were mainly settled by the Formula of Concord of
1580, a rigorous interpretation of the Augsburg Confession. Lutheran theology became learned but un-
original—a "Protestant scholasticism." But in worship, Bible-reading, preaching, and instruction the
people were made vastly more aware of the values of
Christianity than their fathers had been.

14. CALVIN AND THE REFORMED CHURCHES

Zwingli's work in German Switzerland.—Switzerland
grew up from small beginnings in the late thirteenth
century as a federal republic and in the Reformation
era was an increasingly important state. At first its
people had been German-speaking peasant mountain-
eers, but it now possessed also a number of growing
and progressive towns. The worst element in the nation's life was the traffic in mercenary soldiers which
had a demoralizing effect upon the sturdy Swiss man-
hood.

The Protestantism that arose in Switzerland did not
attach itself to Lutheranism but came to form the second or "Reformed" branch of Protestantism. Its first
leader was Huldreich Zwingli (1483–1531), a well-
educated priest who became a careful student of the

Greek New Testament and in 1518 came to Zurich resolved, as he said, "to preach Christ from the fountain." An ardent patriot, he induced the Zurichers to prohibit the recruiting of mercenaries. His scriptural, evangelical, and ethical preaching led to controversy, and his opponents were worsted in a series of public disputations. The success of Luther no doubt encouraged the upgrowth of Protestant opinion under his leadership, though he was personally less indebted to Luther than to Erasmus. On many points his views of reform paralleled those of Luther, but Luther rejected his more radical interpretation of the Lord's Supper. By 1523 the Reformation in Zurich was well begun, and a series of fundamental changes in worship and beliefs soon followed. These were accompanied by much preaching and instruction and supported by the democratic government of Zurich which had long been accustomed to take a hand in church matters. Most of the clergy followed Zwingli's lead, and parish life went on under the new arrangements, with simplified services in the vernacular. So puritanical was Zwingli that at first instrumental and choir music was excluded. Zwingli's writings came to be widely known, and his reforms were soon imitated under like-minded leaders in Basel, St. Gallen, Bern, and other Swiss centers. Opposition arose, however, in the "forest cantons," and blockade measures taken against them by Zurich resulted in an attack upon the Zurichers in which Zwingli was slain (1531). Protestant expansion in German Switzerland was halted;

but Henry Bullinger and other capable men maintained and consolidated the Reformed church. The first Swiss confession was adopted in 1536.

Farel and Calvin in Geneva.—Meanwhile under protection and encouragement from Bern venturesome preachers of reform penetrated the French-speaking areas in the west which were then becoming attached to the Swiss confederacy and of which the chief towns were Neuchâtel, Lausanne, and Geneva. William Farel, an eloquent French convert to Protestantism, entered Geneva and gathered adherents. The city had been in a state of revolt against the already reduced authority of its medieval ruler, who represented the House of Savoy, and it now expelled its bishop, who had attached himself to the Savoy interest against the burghers. Farel and his assistants secured the use of the churches; the clergy took flight, and on May 21, 1536, the citizens solemnly pledged themselves to "live according to the Word of God."

John Calvin (1509–64) was the son of a notary of Noyon. Stimulated from boyhood by able teachers, he had become a brilliant scholar at Paris and mingled humanistic with legal studies at Orléans and Bourges. In association with pupils of Lefèvre who had come under Lutheran influence, and with his cousin, Olivétan, who prepared a French translation of the Bible for the Waldenses, Calvin had experienced a "sudden conversion" (1534?) to the persecuted Protestant cause. He visited several parts of France, interviewed the aged Lefèvre, and went to Basel to complete and publish his *Institutes of the Christian Religion* (1536), the book which in later enlarged editions gave direction to Reformed theology for a century.

After a short stay in Ferrara and an errand to Paris, Calvin, planning to go to Basel to continue his writing, took a night's lodging in Geneva, was invited by Farel and reluctantly consented to join him as professor of Holy Scripture. With Farel he set forth articles for the government of the church which called for strict discipline to guard the sanctity of the communion. The city was now governed by a series of elective councils, of which the Little Council of twenty members and four syndics was most important. The councils supported the new church plan; but resistance to discipline on the part of the free-living wealthier burghers, and the attempt of the Bernese to bring Genevan worship into fuller accord with their own, led to a crisis in which Calvin and Farel left the city (1538).

Calvin's exile, return, and rising power.—Calvin accepted Bucer's invitation to Strassburg, where he taught and wrote and conducted a church of French refugees. The degree of Bucer's influence upon him is not clear, but it must have been considerable. Calvin also attended the conferences of 1540–41 between Lutheran and Roman Catholic theologians and formed a friendship with Melanchthon. Meanwhile partisan strife reigned in Geneva, giving occasion to Cardinal James Sadoleto to exhort the citizens to return to the papal obedience. This called forth from Calvin a brilliant and effective reply. The Genevese now wanted him back, and Calvin yielded to their urgent and repeated appeals. He was to spend the remainder of his life (1541–64) in the strenuous task of making Geneva a reformed city and the nursery of Protestantism in western Europe.

With a committee of the Little Council he prepared the *Ecclesiastical Ordinances*, the church constitution of Geneva. It provided for the careful examination of ministers in life and doctrine and set up a consistory of ministers and lay elders to supervise discipline so that offenders should be excluded from communion and subjected to penances. Severe old statutes which Geneva had left unenforced, and new regulations in accord with the new church order, were employed to maintain a puritan standard of behavior among the people. Only gradually, however, was Calvin able to win the full assent of the government and people to his plan. He met with opposition from parties representing some of the leading families who resented the discipline and from individuals who opposed his teaching. By measures that were in some cases harsh, opponents were silenced or sent away. The Spanish radical physician, Michael Servetus, who had previously been in controversy with Calvin, and had recently escaped from a prison of the Inquisition, was burned at the stake in Geneva (1553). His death was the gravest blot upon Calvin's regime, although the manner of it was not of Calvin's choosing, for he wanted Servetus beheaded. It came at a time when Calvin's authority was imperiled by the election of magistrates unfavorable to him. Calvin has been called a dictator; but he never used his position of leadership to impair the city's system of elective government. At any time he might have been dismissed, and indeed at certain crises he expected to be, by the elected councils. At their request he had already employed his legal knowledge to revise the laws of Geneva, and his revised code was later praised by liberal political thinkers.

Calvin and the Geneva theocracy.—By 1555 all serious opposition was overcome. Calvin was now the most effective leader of Protestantism. From his pen came a flood of writings—tracts, letters, learned commentaries on the books of the Bible—all marked by literary distinction, whether written in French or in Latin. From the beginning he had given attention to education, and in 1558 he established the Academy of Geneva which became an educational center for the training of preachers and teachers who were to spread his gospel in France, the Netherlands, and other countries.

During the fifties a large number of foreign refugees settled temporarily or permanently in Geneva. An English colony, in flight from Queen Mary's persecutions, maintained its own church under the leadership of John Knox and John Goodman. Many of the French-speaking refugees became citizens and added strength to Calvin's cause.

Calvin's teachings and discipline were such as to produce a vigorous type of Christian character. He regarded his own conversion as a commitment to the will of God as revealed in the Scriptures, and he related all human affairs intimately to the Divine will. His theology centered in the sovereignty of God, which involved the predestination to salvation, or else the reprobation, of every man. The elect embraced God's will and expressed their faith through a devotion to the cause of God in the world as well as through spiritual worship. He taught a high doctrine of the church as the communion of saints extended through the world, one, catholic, and holy. To make men fit for this high fellowship he imposed his austere discipline. The simple and impressive worship included much singing of psalms in French; able composers provided the tunes, and the children were carefully trained to sing.

Calvin's emphasis on communion went far beyond the community of Geneva and found expression in his many efforts to bring about the unification of Protestantism. He formed an agreement with the German Swiss church (1549), kept in touch with the rising Protestant churches of France, and inspired the movement which later gave Protestantism to the Netherlands. The Scottish Reformation, too, while aided by Lutheran and Zwinglian influences, owed a great debt to Calvin. Calvinism spread into the German Rhine cities; it came to be adopted in the Palatinate and other German states and by many of the nobles of Bohemia and Hungary. But the Counter Reformation gradually checked this expansion. After a series of civil wars in which religious and political opposition to the Valois rulers of France were combined, Henry IV, the Calvinist successor of the last Valois, decided for the sake of peace to adopt the Roman Catholic faith. But, in the Edict of Nantes (1598), he gave to the Reformed church a large measure of toleration.

The spread and influence of Calvinism.—French Calvinism achieved national organization in the midst of severe persecution in 1559, adopting a confession largely prepared by Calvin and a plan of government and discipline suitable to its national extent. In the Netherlands Calvinism became the religion of the patriotic movement under William of Orange (d. 1584) which freed seven northern provinces from Spanish rule and established the Dutch Republic. The Reformed church in the Netherlands was closely related to the state and followed in its organization the provincial outlines, with occasional meetings of national synods. Its confession of faith is known as the Belgic Confession (1566). Both the French and the Dutch Calvinists had efficient schools and a strong intellectual life. About the beginning of the seventeenth century the whole Reformed church was greatly stirred by a controversy in the Netherlands over predestination and free will, in which the liberal followers of Arminius (d. 1609) were pronounced heretics by the dominant rigorist party.

The Reformed churches everywhere emphasized education, but in the earlier generations their intellectual interests were largely confined to theology and political theory. They were disliked and opposed by absolute rulers; and in turn they produced the leading political opponents of absolutism and advocates of a conservative type of representative government. Through its intellectual life and its social activism as well as through its sturdy piety, Calvinism deeply and permanently affected European culture and has remained an unspent force to the present era. Some modern writers have pointed to the fact that Calvinism was most generally adopted by the business classes and ascribed to it the the chief part in the rise of capitalism and the capitalist spirit. It is true that Calvin, working in a city of some business importance, was more favorable to business than Luther; but he was exceedingly careful to guard against any encouragement of greed. He "cared nothing for money," and if he taught industry and thrift it was not to foster the rise of a profit system but to enable those who practiced these "middle-class virtues" the more effectively to serve their fellows. But much of later "Calvinism" has deviated from Calvin's own teaching and discipline.

15. THE REFORMATION IN THE BRITISH ISLES

National differences.—In the Middle Ages not only were England and Scotland separate kingdoms but they were also inveterate enemies. The Stuart kings of Scotland had long maintained an alliance with France, with which nation England was frequently at war; and the borders of England and Scotland saw many a battle. Yet the two peoples shared to some extent a common culture. Both Chaucer and Wyclif were influential in Scotland, and Scottish scholars were numerous at the English universities. Gradually it came to be felt in both nations that a friendlier relationship would be advantageous; and the Reformation was accompanied by the cementing of this friendship, though not the complete obliteration of the old hostilities. Even after the Stuarts succeeded to the English

Tudors in 1603, the nations remained separate for a century, and the national churches have retained to the present day the characteristic differences then assumed.

Tyndale and the English Bible.—It was under Henry VIII (1509–47), the second Tudor king, that the English Reformation began. Early in Henry's reign Erasmus was at Cambridge, and John Colet, dean of St. Paul's, was urging reform in the education and morals of the clergy. At the same time a considerable number of readers of Wyclif's Bible and sermons were being persecuted for heresy. In the twenties a group of Cambridge men led by Thomas Bilney began to preach an evangelical message learned from the Scriptures. Many young Englishmen felt the influence of Luther, whom Henry had vigorously condemned. Of these the most important was William Tyndale, of Gloucestershire, a priest and a capable scholar, who translated the New Testament from the Greek version of Erasmus, published it abroad (1525), and had it brought to England by sympathetic merchants. In a few years he had completed six books of the Old Testament, and he later carefully revised his translations. These English versions were accompanied by argumentative prologues and notes, and they were eagerly read despite the efforts of the authorities to suppress them. Many of the books, and some of the men who circulated them, were burned. Tyndale himself had to depend on Englishmen in the Netherlands for his protection. One of these betrayed him, and he was strangled and burned by the emperor's officers near Brussels (1536). But the

Bible in English could not be suppressed, and already a version dependent in large degree upon Tyndale's had appeared (1535); and others were soon to appear under authorization by Henry and his ministers. In 1537 the bishop of Hereford warned his episcopal colleagues with reference to the translated Bible: "Think ye not that we can by any sophistical subtleties steal out of the world again the light that every man doth see."

Henry VIII as head of the church.—Meanwhile by the king's action the English church had been severed from the papal jurisdiction. The pope's control of the church had been greatly reduced by acts of the English parliament in the fourteenth century, and the steps taken by Henry, startling as they were, may be regarded as the completion of a long process. Henry, having no male heir, was anxious for the succession of his line and doubted the validity of his marriage to Catharine of Aragon, his brother's widow. When he became infatuated with Anne Boleyn, he determined to secure the annulment of his marriage. The ambitious and ostentatious Cardinal Thomas Wolsey was Henry's chief minister. Wolsey was appointed with a legate from Rome to try the case; but Pope Clement VII kept the decision in suspense, and Wolsey died under a charge of treason. A series of antipapal acts, proposed by Henry and willingly adopted by parliament, culminated in the repudiation of the papal authority and the assumption by the king of the title "Supreme Head of the Church of England" (1534).

Thomas Cranmer (1489–1556), son of a Nottinghamshire yeoman, and a Cambridge scholar, had been appointed archbishop of Canterbury (1533). He had long been opposed to the papal power, and on the king's errands abroad he had become familiar with Lutheranism. Cranmer lent himself to the dissolution of Henry's marriage with Catharine, which he believed to be invalid, and furthered the marriage with Anne. He favored the English Bible and slowly reached a Protestant position in theology. Thomas Cromwell, an unscrupulous politician, now the king's chief minister, was given large authority in church affairs. Under his direction a drastic policy of the extermination of the monasteries, some of which had been earlier suppressed, was carried through. The monks were pensioned, and many of them received church appointments; but the few who resisted were harshly treated, and some of them perished. John Fisher, bishop of Rochester, and Thomas More, the devout humanist who had been active against Tyndale and his friends, were put to death for resisting the king's policy. Henry never became a Protestant, and his harsh laws cost the lives of persons attached to both religious parties. Cromwell himself, who had grown too important and had displeased the king, was beheaded (1540). While many of Henry's laws and deeds were tyrannical, his persecutions were not extensive. He refused to punish Cranmer on charges raised by the archbishop's enemies. Before he died he appointed a council to guide the realm in the minority of his son, Edward VI, which contained a number of known supporters of Protestantism.

The Reformation in Edward's reign.—In Edward's

reign (1547–53) the Reformation advanced. While Somerset held power (until 1550) Cranmer was able to give direction to its progress. The Book of Common Prayer was compiled by him. The 1549 edition was followed by the more Protestant Prayer-Book of 1552, which, with slight changes under Elizabeth, became the book of worship of many generations of Englishmen. Cranmer also wrote the Articles of Religion, which formed the basis of the later Thirty-nine Articles, the Anglican statement of the faith. But Northumberland was now in power. A man of no religious convictions, he promoted reform only in order to control church property and pursued reckless political courses. At Edward's death he tried to place Lady Jane Grey, who was married to his son, upon the throne; and he completed his hypocrisies by professing Roman Catholicism at his execution.

While the changes in the English church were attended by the heartless greed and cruelty of some political leaders who seized the church's wealth, they also gave opportunity for the advance of popular religion. In Edward's reign numerous preachers and reforming bishops labored to bring the people under the influence of the Gospel. One of the most gifted of the preachers was Hugh Latimer, whose witty sermons have a place in English literature. Nicholas Ridley, bishop of London, promoted discipline, education, and charity in his diocese. John Hooper was a radical Protestant and a forerunner of Puritanism. Numerous foreign Protestant scholars found refuge and opportunity in England. These included Martin Bucer of Strassburg, Jan

Laski of Poland, Peter Martyr Vermigli of Italy, and
Vallerand Poullain of France. John Knox, the Scottish reformer, spent four active years in England,
chiefly in the north. Cranmer planned for a Protestant
conference with Melanchthon and Calvin as members;
but the death of Edward put an end to this project.

Mary and Elizabeth.—Queen Mary (1553–58), the
daughter of Catharine of Aragon, combined the iron
will of the Tudors with the faith and intolerance of the
Spanish house and came to power embittered by ad-
versity. She was determined to restore England to its
old relation with the papacy. She married Philip II of
Spain, who, indifferent to her affection and disliked in
England, busied himself with Continental affairs and
was anything but an attentive husband. Her archbishop and chief adviser was Cardinal Reginald Pole,
whose mother had been put to death by Henry and
who came from a long residence abroad, unable to
realize the degree in which Englishmen had adopted
the Reformation. Mary obtained the acceptance of
her plans by parliament, restored the papal authority
and the medieval laws against heresy, and entered
upon a course of fanatical persecution in which more
than two hundred and seventy leaders and followers
of the Protestant cause were sent to the flames. Among
these were Hooper, Latimer, Ridley, and Cranmer.
At the same time hundreds of Protestants, clergy and
laity, found refuge on the Continent. Some of these
Marian exiles became on their return the founders of
Puritanism; others became leaders of the Elizabethan
church in which they strengthened the antagonism to
Rome.

The Settlement of Religion by various measures in the early years of Elizabeth (1558–1603) gave permanent form to Anglicanism. Under the revised Prayer-Book and the Articles uniformity was demanded; but Elizabeth was no zealous persecutor and the ecclesiastical policy was moderate. Its real aim was to include as many Englishmen as possible within the national church. But there were opposing parties on the right and on the left. Most of the numerous adherents of the medieval forms of worship reluctantly conformed, and those who did not were penalized by fines. A few active supporters of the papacy, led by a group of Jesuits, suffered death for treason. On the other hand, groups of Puritans who formed separatist congregations were forcibly suppressed or compelled to emigrate. A party who sought to give the church a presbyterian constitution obtained some support in parliament, but its progress was checked. Distinguished theological scholars, such as John Jewel and Richard Hooker, ably defended Anglican principles against all opponents. Long before the end of Elizabeth's reign it became apparent that the church as legally established was approved by the great majority of the people. The literary renaissance of Shakespeare's age led men's interests away from theological controversy. But the discontented minority were not fully assimilated to the church, and there were again Puritan exiles on the Continent who would help to inspire in England a later religious and political revolution.

The Scottish Reformation.—The medieval Scottish church had accumulated a disproportionate share of the country's limited wealth. Most of the clergy were quite unfit for their tasks and had lost the respect of the people. There were a few Lollards (Wycliffites) in Scotland at the opening of the century. Tyndale's New Testament was a factor there also, and people called "New Testamenters" were punished for reading it under King James V (1513–42). In 1528 young Patrick Hamilton, who in studies abroad had felt the influence of Erasmus and Luther, was burned at St. Andrews for preaching Reformation doctrine. George Wishart, who had known Latimer at Cambridge and had adopted Zwingli's views on the Continent, after a preaching tour in Scotland suffered under Cardinal David Beaton in 1546. John Knox (1513–72) first came to be known as an associate of Wishart.

Beaton represented the papal cause and the French alliance and had many enemies. Soon after Wishart's death he was slain by a group of nobles, who afterward defended themselves for a time against the French in the Castle of St. Andrews, and were joined by Protestants seeking protection. Here Knox began to preach. The castle fell, and he with others was taken as a galley slave by the French. Mary of Guise, widow of James V, with the aid of Beaton, had secured the repudiation by Scotland of an agreement that her baby daughter Mary should marry Edward, Henry VIII's heir, and had sent the child to her relatives in France. The English made two destructive invasions of Scotland in vain efforts to reverse this action. But many Scots held Beaton and the French responsible for this and looked for an English alliance. Despite a good deal of persecution, but with the favor of some of the leading nobles, Scottish Protestantism grew. When Elizabeth came to the English throne, a Protestant and anti-French revolt was in progress in Scotland. Knox returned to the country and inspired the movement by his exhortations. Elizabeth, though she disliked Knox, sent needed aid to the rebels, and the French were obliged to make peace and leave Scotland. Knox and his associates were now free to organize a national Reformed church (1560).

They drew up the First Scots Confession, a simple statement of Reformed Protestantism, and a Book of Discipline setting forth the structure of the church and proposing a complete reform of education. The Confession was adopted by the parliament, but the adoption of the Book of Discipline was prevented by greedy nobles because they wanted for themselves properties that were to be used to support the schools. Yet in part the proposed discipline was carried out in afteryears at the direction of the general assembly of ministers and elders. Under this national council of the church there came to be formed synods, presbyteries, and church sessions, a graded series of representative councils for church government. A similar conciliar organization was arising in French and in Dutch Calvinism.

This Scottish presbyterianism was organized despite the resistance of the young Queen Mary, now (1561) returned from France. Later there was an attempt to give something like Anglican episcopacy to the Scottish church, and some time afterward this was countered by an effort to make the Church of England presbyterian (1643–48). Both movements equally failed, but they left some Episcopalians in Scotland and some Presbyterians in England.

The Reformation in Ireland.—From the twelfth century Ireland was subject to the English kings, but outside the "Pale"—a narrow province around Dublin— English influence was limited. The Irish people, with their own peculiarities and discords, felt no desire for an antipapal Reformation. Henry VIII appointed bishops for Ireland who favored a religious policy such as he was following in England, and he induced an Irish parliament to declare him "of the Church of England and of Ireland on earth the Supreme Head" (1540). Later the English Prayer-Book was authorized; but, since to most of the Irish people English was a foreign language, the book proved unacceptable to them. Queen Mary, of course, reversed this policy but failed to pacify Ireland. Elizabeth, in her efforts to check rebellion and turbulence in Ireland, mingled severity with conciliation. She gave the Irish a Latin and an Irish version of the Prayer-Book. Yet dislike of the English power and loyalty to the pope remained characteristic of the majority of Irishmen, and only a few were attracted to the Reformation.

Queen Mary began the policy of "plantation" or settlement of English families in expropriated Irish lands; and this method was employed by James I on a large scale in what is called the "plantation of Ulster." The newcomers were Anglicans from England and Presbyterians from Scotland. The (Anglican) Church of Ireland received fresh strength by this migration and at the same time profited by the leadership of the scholarly and conciliatory James Usher, archbishop of Armagh (d. 1656). Another result of the plantation was the organization of a vigorous Presbyterian church in Ulster. Descendants of these "Scotch-Irish" Presbyterians were later to form an important element in the American colonies.

16. LEFT-WING RELIGIOUS MOVEMENTS
THE COUNTER REFORMATION

The Anabaptists.—Two widely divergent aspects of the Reformation era remain to be treated—the leftist groups and the revival of the papal church. Some of the numerous left-wing group movements were indebted to pre-Reformation sects and found their opportunity rather than their origin in the controversies concerning Protestantism. This is true of the Anabaptists, who were apparently indebted to the Franciscan Spirituals and to a variety of pre-Lutheran scriptural and mystical heretical sects. Early in the twenties of the century they appeared in considerable numbers in Switzerland, Germany, and the Netherlands, and were soon spread by both persecution and propagation through parts of all European countries.

Under the name "Anabaptist" we discover a variety of religious opinion and practice rather than an integrated movement; but some principles were common to most of the persons and groups so designated. They sought a return to primitive Christianity and repudiated the whole upgrowth of church institutions and relationships of the patristic and medieval periods. They tended to reject all distinction between clergy and laity and all traditional forms of worship and sacraments. Convinced that infant baptism was unscriptural they practiced believers' baptism only. With a literal adherence to Scripture they often combined an individualistic doctrine of "inner light." Where they had opportunity, as, for a time in parts of Moravia, they adopted a highly organized economic communism. They were generally unwilling to participate in politics and taught absolute opposition to war. But a large element of them espoused apocalyptic doctrines which led them into violence. A revolutionary situation in Münster, Westphalia, gave opportunity for thousands of Anabaptists to congregate there to await the second coming of Christ. They seized the city and when attacked defended themselves vigorously with the sword, until they were crushed, with much loss of life (1535). The greatly disproportionate number of women in the besieged town partly accounts for the adoption of polygamy by the defenders, a lapse which nowhere else appears in Anabaptist history.

Most of the rank and file of the Anabaptists were townsfolk of the poorer class, but most leaders of the movement were capable scholars. Conrad Grebel (d. 1526) was the well-educated son of a Zurich merchant; Balthasar Hubmaier (burnt 1528) was a former professor of theology at Ingoldstadt; Pilgram Marbeck (d. 1556), while not a scholar, was a distinguished engineer of Augsburg and Strassburg; Menno Simons (d. 1561) was a Frisian priest before becoming one of the founders of the Mennonites. These teachers of revolutionary doctrines were nevertheless sober and thoughtful men. But the movement had a fanatical fringe, represented by such violent agitators as Thomas Münzer (executed 1525), who ferociously exhorted the revolting German peasants, and Melchior Hoffmann (d. 1543), the popular preacher of a lurid apocalypticism. At the opposite pole from these stands the tolerant humanist and mystic Hans Denck (d. 1527), who in his short life gave moderate guidance to many adherents of the movement.

The Anabaptists held the true church to be the assembly of believers, not the organ for religion of the people as a whole. The idea of a state church was repugnant to them. Their doctrines were accordingly condemned by all the state-connected churches, and, except at Strassburg and in parts of Moravia, they were bitterly persecuted as dangerous radicals.

The Socinians.—Another leftist movement was Socinianism, with which may be coupled the earlier antitrinitarianism of Michael Servetus (see above, p. 113). In two works on the Trinity (1531–32) Servetus denied the unity of the three Persons and the eternal sonship of Christ. It may have been under the influence of Laelius Socinus (1525–62) that Bernardino Ochino (1487–1564) adopted in his late years an antitrinitarian position. Both men were from Siena, and they were associated in Switzerland. Similar views on the Trinity were held by Anabaptist groups in Poland and Italy. The application of the name Socinianism to the antitrinitarian movement is due mainly to the work of

Faustus Socinus (1539–1604), a nephew of Laelius, who probably derived some of his ideas from his uncle. Laelius in his youth was a member of a liberal group at Vicenza which was suppressed by the Inquisition. Laelius crossed the Alps and made the acquaintance of Calvin, Melanchthon, and Bullinger. His wide travels included a visit to Poland, the later scene of his nephew's labors. He made no decisive statement of anti-trinitarian opinions, but his questioning spirit gave anxiety to Calvin. With Bullinger he was more friendly, and his death took place in Zurich.

Faustus was privately educated in Siena, and his mind was saturated with Renaissance thought. After a period in France and Geneva he settled in Florence and began to write. Twelve years later, tired of compromise with Roman Catholicism, he left Italy to study and work out his theology. His book *On Jesus Christ the Savior* appeared in 1578. The last twenty-five years of his life were spent in Poland, where another Italian unitarian, George Blandrata, had preceded him. A large number of sects had arisen in Poland, but these were now losing ground through the activity of the Jesuits. Certain nobles befriended Socinus; but in his effort to propagate his views and to unite his followers he experienced much danger. He succeeded in creating a group of churches in Poland and Transylvania; but this organized Socinianism was almost extinguished by persecution after his death. As an intellectual leaven, however, Socianism lived on.

The Protestant Reformers had seen no objection to the creeds of the early church and believed the traditional trinitarianism to be in accord with Scripture. Socinus, like the Anabaptists, interpreted the New Testament without any preference for patristic dogma. He modified the accepted belief about Christ mainly at two points. For him Christ's death was significant not as a propitiatory sacrifice but as exercising a moral influence upon man. And he held that Jesus was not eternally the Son of God but became immortal at his resurrection. The very admission to discussion of such doctrines was a menace to the security of the Protestant confessions with their reaffirmations of the old creeds. Socinus also opposed all persecution for religious opinions. Dutch and English exponents of these and related ideas transmitted a Socinian trend to later liberal thought. The Socinians were early called Unitarians, and some of Socinus' teachings have been influential in modern Unitarianism.

Unattached mystics and tolerationists.—Amid the interchurch controversies of the time stood a series of unattached thinkers who taught a mystical doctrine of "inner light" coupled with a broad liberalism and tolerance. Thus Sebastian Franck (1499–1539), a Swabian, who felt the influence of Denck at Nürnberg, affirmed: "The inner light is nothing else than the Word of God"; and again: "Nobody is the master of my faith and I desire to be the master of nobody's faith. I love any man whom I can help." More mystical and contemplative was Valentin Weigel (1533–88), who, rejecting "external revelation," made religion to consist of an inner quiet of the soul responsive to divine promptings, and conceived of Christ as "the head of a divine humanity" and of the church as the invisible body of those "conformed to Christ and his cross." Through John Arndt and Jacob Böhme this strain of liberal mysticism was mediated to Philip Jacob Spener and the Pietists of the late seventeenth century. The affinities of this type of thought with Quakerism are apparent.

Besides these tolerant mystics there arose a series of advocates of toleration who, partly under the influence of Erasmus, repudiated all persecution as un-Christian. Prominent among these was Sebastian Castellio (1515–63), who had assisted Calvin but disagreed with him and later published a *Treatise on Heretics* (1554) advocating a Christian considerateness against the prevailing cruelty of persecution. Similar was the position of Jacob Acontius (d. 1566), an Italian who wrote in Switzerland and in England. In his book *The Stratagems of Satan* (1565) he denounced creeds in general as a cause of persecution. Of the many other advocates of toleration some, however, argued mainly from the standpoint of political expediency rather than from that of religious principle.

The Counter Reformation.—Though Protestantism and the radical sects had entered all parts of Europe, many strong governments still maintained their connection with the papacy and sternly resisted the new movements. Soon after the beginning of the Reformation a revival of devotion within the Roman church manifested itself in the rise of new, and the reform of old, ascetic orders. Important among these movements were the Theatines (1524), composed of earnest priests, and the Capuchins (1525), a reformed group of Franciscans who were active as popular preachers in Italy and later in France.

But the greatest of these new orders was the Society of Jesus, founded by Ignatius Loyola (1491–1556), a former Spanish soldier who, while still a layman, pledged to his cause a few select disciples at the University of Paris and in 1540 obtained the sanction of his organization by Pope Paul III. At first the Jesuits were limited to sixty members, but they were soon permitted to expand as they chose. They attracted able recruits and numbered in their membership eminent theologians. They were obligated to serve the pope wherever he might send them and, no less, to obey unquestioningly their own general. Although difficulties between the general and the pope occasionally arose, the Society yielded incomparable service to the strengthening of the papacy. Diego Lainez largely determined the theological decisions of the Council of Trent and succeeded Ignatius as general. Francis Xavier led a short but brilliant mission in the Far East. Peter Canisius became the apostle of the revival in Germany. The Jesuits employed their energies in the education of youth, gave personal guidance to members of the nobility and to princes, and exercised an important political influence on behalf of their church.

Pope Paul III (1534–49) cautiously undertook measures of reform. He received an alarming report on the condition of the church (1538) from a committee of cardinals whom he had appointed to office for their reforming interests. He established the Roman Inquisition (1542) which destroyed the Protestant groups in Italy. He finally secured agreement with the emperor on the long-disputed question of a general council, and called the Council of Trent. This council was in session during three periods between 1545 and 1563 and was adroitly managed by the papal legates. Three-quarters of those who signed its documents were Italians. Its canons and decrees constituted a new basis for Roman Catholicism comparable to the confessions of the Protestant churches but specifically rejecting the leading Protestant doctrines. It reaffirmed medieval teachings on purgatory and indulgences but abolished many scandalous abuses. Disregarding the work of the humanists on the Greek and Hebrew scriptures, the council reinstated the Latin Bible as authoritative. After its close the index of prohibited books which it had prepared (a revision of an earlier papal index), containing a statement of the classes of forbidden writings and a list of titles, was published. The Roman Catechism (1566) lucidly summarized the doctrines of Trent, and a number of more elementary catechisms came into use. Armed with these instruments of instruction and repression, and led by Jesuit and other scholars and propagandists, the church recovered much lost ground and became once more a powerful factor in European life.

CHAPTER V

THE HISTORY OF EASTERN
ORTHODOXY

17. THE BYZANTINE CHURCH TO THE
GREAT SCHISM, A.D. 1054

Losses sustained by the Byzantine church.—When its institutional organization was fully developed (in 451),
the total Christian church was divided into five patriarchates, namely: Rome, Constantinople, Alexandria,
Antioch, and Jerusalem. The four last named comprised the Eastern or Byzantine church, while Rome
dominated the West.

The formula of the Council Chalcedon was not favorably received by all groups of Christians. Those who rejected it did so for various reasons. Among the reasons
may be named nascent nationalism, mutual suspicions,
personal jealousies and ambitions, misunderstandings,
and genuine religious convictions. Since the formula
represented a victory of the patriarch of Constantinople
over the more ancient patriarchate of Alexandria, as
well as the defeat of what the Alexandrians regarded as
the teaching of their famous patriarch, Cyril; and since
the Council deposed the reigning Alexandrian patriarch, Dioscurus; it is not difficult to understand why
Egypt identified itself with the cause of monophysitism
(the Greek word meaning "one nature," i.e., the doc-

135

trine that Jesus Christ had only divine, not divine-human, nature). The Egyptians established a separate church, the Coptic church, which was regarded by the Orthodox group as heretical. This became the national church of Egypt and as such has survived to this day. The conquest of Egypt by the Arabs in 642 was facilitated by the spirit of opposition to the imperial rule felt by most Egyptians. By it Egypt was cut off both politically and religiously from the Empire.

Egypt was followed in this regard by its daughter-churches, Nubia and Ethiopia (Abyssinia). The Nubian church ultimately disappeared altogether, but the Abyssinian people remained in close dependence upon the Coptic church down to our times. In fact, the head of the Ethiopian church was always a Copt, appointed by the Coptic patriarch.

A similar situation prevailed in Palestine and Syria. Jerusalem had been raised to the rank of patriarchate by the Council of Chalcedon. It could be expected that this would insure its loyalty. But the contrary was the fact. The newly created patriarch, Juvenal, found the gates of Jerusalem closed against him and was accused of "apostasy." He was obliged to return to Constantinople to request the escort of the imperial cohorts and then to make his "triumphal entry" into Jerusalem in a most un-Christlike fashion. Despite the temporary ascendancy of the Chalcedonian doctrine which was procured by the use of force, the people of Palestine ultimately became predominantly monophysite.

Even more surprising is the case of Syria, which was dominated ecclesiastically by the patriarchate of Antioch. Despite the fact that the Antiochene theology had been traditionally strongly opposed to the Alexandrian, in the end the monophysite influence secured the upper hand. The resentment against Chalcedon may have been fostered largely by a sense of nationalistic opposition to the Greek domination of the Byzantine church or by the fact that the Council of Chalcedon had dealt roughly with the territories of the Antiochene patriarchate; for the two newly created patriarchates, those of Constantinople and of Jerusalem, had been carved out of the territory of the former. At any rate, Syria in the end became predominantly monophysite. Both Palestine and Syria were among the first conquests of the Arabs in the thirties of the seventh century. Separated from the Empire as well as from the Byzantine church, these two communions have perpetuated themselves as separate groups to this day.

The Nestorian group, which comprised the bulk of the far eastern Syrian churches of the territories dominated by Edessa, in northwestern Mesopotamia, suffered a great deal of persecution by the imperial Greek church ever since the condemnation of Nestorius by the Council of Ephesus in 431. Because of this persecution, a great number of the leaders sought refuge in the neighboring Persia. They were able to organize a strong and vital church, which in self-protection was constrained to emphasize its differences from the Orthodox Byzantine church, of which the patriarch of Constantinople was the leading hierarch. Otherwise, the Persian government was likely to suspect their church of political disloyalty. It was this church which in the course of time became imbued with a missionary zeal beyond any other. Some time in the sixth century this "great church of the East" sent out missionaries to the Malabar coast of India, where they founded or re-established a Christian community known as that of St. Thomas. This is the oldest native Christian community in India and persists to this day.

Furthermore, the Nestorian Christians penetrated to central China in the first half of the seventh century and gained there a small number of adherents. According to the testimonial of a Chinese monument, set up in 781 in or near the capital of China, Ch'angan, Christianity became influential, was organized under a metropolitan, and produced some literature. After the extinction of this body, Nestorianism was again introduced into China, after having penetrated even among the Tartar and Turkish tribes, especially the Uighurs and the Onguts of the former race and the Keraits of the latter. Both are said in the thirteenth century to have been Christians. The mother of Kublai Khan, the famous ruler of the vast Mongol Empire, was a Nestorian Christian, a Kerait princess.

Gains.—The imperial Byzantine church which suffered all these losses made up for them by expansion north into the Balkans and into Russia. The Balkan peninsula had developed, during the first three centuries of the Christian Era, a fair degree of Latin civilization. But, beginning with the fourth century, it was successively invaded by various Gothic tribes, such as the Ostrogoths and the Visigoths; later, the various Slavic tribes, such as the ancestors of modern Bulgarians, Serbians, and Croatians, took their place. In the process of conquering the land, they all but destroyed the ancient civilization and the newly established Christianity. Thus the Balkans reverted to paganism and had to be reconverted to Christianity. The process was begun in Bulgaria, where Christianity was introduced in the days of the czar Boris, who was baptized in 863. After a long struggle on the part of the Byzantine church, particularly during the reign of Patriarch Photius, against the competing efforts of the Western church under the leadership of Pope Nicholas I, Bulgaria finally chose Constantinople as its ecclesiastical superior. During the glorious reign of the Bulgarian czar Simeon (893–927), the Bulgarian church reached a considerable degree of culture. It produced a native literature as well as many translations from the Greek. It was this literature in the native Slavic, at present designated "church Slavonic," which then spread to other Slavic countries converted to Christianity and served there as the nucleus of native Christian culture.

Sporadic efforts had been made, from the ninth century onward, to evangelize the Serbians. But this work did not meet with permanent success. It was not until the Grand Zhupan, Stephen Nemanya (1168–95), succeeded in seizing control over the majority of Serbian territories that the ecclesiastical unification was effected. Being himself a fervent adherent of Eastern Orthodoxy, he proclaimed that form of Christianity the state church.

The organizer of the independent Serbian national

church was Stephen's youngest son, who is generally known under his monastic name, Sava. After the conquest of Constantinople (1204) by the Western princes who led the Fourth Crusade, and the virtual destruction of the Byzantine Empire in the Balkans, the Serbian Orthodox church was in great danger of succumbing to Latin influences. It was under these grave conditions that Sava, then the head of the Serbian monastery of Khilandar on Mount Athos, returned to his native country. Realizing the danger which threatened the Serbian church from Rome, Sava secured for his church from the ecumenical patriarch, Manuel, the rank of an independent archbishopric. Thereupon, he himself was consecrated the "first archbishop of all the Serbian lands." He then organized the church on a thoroughly national basis.

Another major gain of the Byzantine church was secured in the conversion of Russia to Christianity. But this subject will be treated later.

Causes leading to the Great Schism.—Until the Great Schism of 1054, the Christian church, at least in theory, was one. Despite many subsidiary schisms, most of which were short lived, the eastern and western halves of Christendom remained in communion with each other.

But there were many causes of division. First of all, there was the linguistic and cultural dissimilarity. Originally, the dominant language of the entire gentile Christian church was Greek. This language was spoken even in Rome down to the middle of the third century. But, gradually, the patriarchate of Rome became altogether Latin-speaking. With the successive deterioration of culture in the West, owing to the barbaric invasions, the knowledge of Greek became a rare accomplishment for Westerners.

As for the East, Latin remained the language of the government until the reign of Justinian I (527–65). Nevertheless, as time went on, Greek became exclusively the language of culture, of government, and of common intercourse. In this way the two branches of the church found it difficult to understand each other. As a consequence they became culturally estranged. Moreover, during the so-called Dark Ages, while the barbaric nations of western Europe were assimilating the ancient Roman culture, the general cultural level was necessarily low. The Byzantine Greek culture did not suffer the calamity which had overtaken the Latins; consequently, by the time of the Great Schism, the culture of the East was incomparably higher than that of the West.

The political situation also contributed to this estrangement. In 325 Emperor Constantine chose the city of Byzantium as the new capital of the Empire, thus definitely abandoning the old capital, Rome. Accordingly, the political center of the Empire was shifted to the East. Moreover, by the successive invasions of the barbarians, the western half was gradually lost to the Empire. This process culminated, in 476, in what is generally designated as the "fall of the Roman Empire." Henceforth, the Roman emperors residing in Constantinople exercised no effective control over the West, except for a short period during the reign of

Justinian I. By the year 800, when Charlemagne was crowned emperor of the Holy Roman Empire by Pope Leo III, the process of political separation of East and West was completed.

In the third place, religious causes contributed to this result. There were many incidents in the ecclesiastical and religious spheres which offered an occasion for a schism between the Eastern and Western churches. One of these was the iconoclastic controversy, which was occasioned by the order of Emperor Leo III prohibiting the worship of images. The struggle broke out in 725 and was not finally settled until 842, when the party favoring the worship of images won the day. During a part of this period, the East and West were out of communion with each other, for the latter consistently upheld image worship.

One of the major schisms occurred during the patriarchate of Photius, who had been chosen and consecrated to his office in an irregular way in 858. Pope Nicholas I refused to recognize Photius as patriarch because the latter would not admit Nicholas' claim to the primacy of the Roman see over all the other patriarchates. The result of mutual recriminations was a schism which lasted until 898.

The Great Schism occurred in 1054 and since that time has definitely divided Christendom. The causes of this schism were complex, but the most important was the rivalry between Pope Leo IX and Patriarch Michael Cerularius. The pope represented the so-called Cluniac reform, which strove to assert the independence of the church from the state. By the very aims of this movement, the pope felt constrained to affirm the supreme jurisdiction of the Roman see over the whole church. Cerularius, on his part, was an ambitious prelate, proud of the commanding influence of his see in the Byzantine Empire. To him, the idea of submitting to the papal claim of universal jurisdiction was utterly abhorrent. In 1053 Leo sent an embassy to Constantinople which arrived the next year. Cerularius refused to deal with the Roman legates. After the death of Leo, which occurred on April 19, 1054, Cerularius claimed that they no longer had authority to represent the papacy. Feeling that their mission proved ineffective, the legates finally decided upon formally breaking off all relations with the patriarch of Constantinople and all his adherents. On July 15, 1054, they repaired to the magnificent basilica of St. Sophia and deposited there a bull of excommunication of Cerularius and all his adherents, condemning him "along with all heretics, together with the devil and his angels." Thus was consummated the division of Christendom which has persisted to this day.

18. THE BYZANTINE CHURCH FROM THE SCHISM TO THE DOWNFALL OF THE EMPIRE

The Crusades.—The Christian East did not look upon the Great Schism as a calamity. Patriarch Cerularius undoubtedly regarded it as a personal victory over Pope Leo IX. The rest of the Orthodox East did not seem to be much impressed, for the contemporary chroniclers and historians hardly mentioned the event.

Nevertheless, it proved to be the beginning of the downfall of the Byzantine church.

Of course, no one could foresee the misfortunes which the future had in store for the Empire. But in 1071 the Byzantine army was defeated for the first time by the Turkish invaders at the Battle of Manzikert. The Turks, thereafter, established themselves permanently in Asia Minor. The pilgrims to the holy places of Palestine were no longer left unmolested and free as they had been previously. The new Turkish masters plundered, maltreated, and in many cases killed them. Moreover, the Turkish menace threatened to attack, and possibly subjugate, the Empire.

Under these circumstances, Emperor Alexius I was willing to accept military aid from the West in the form of mercenary armies under his command. But this appeal was utilized by Pope Urban II for his own purposes. In order to regain prestige for the papacy which had been lost during the struggle of Pope Gregory VII with Emperor Henry IV, Urban, at Clairmont, made an urgent appeal for a crusading army which would rescue the holy places from the hands of the infidels. His call was enthusiastically responded to, and thus the crusading movement was inaugurated in 1095.

When the northern French, Provençal, and Norman nobles, who were leading the crusade, appeared with their armies before Constantinople, Alexius greeted them with mixed emotions. He did not intend to fight the Turks for the benefit of the land-hungry western barons. Accordingly, he demanded an oath of fealty

from them, specifying that whatever territories formerly belonging to the Empire should be recovered from
the Turks, must be returned to the Empire. But this
was not exactly what the crusading leaders expected to
do. When Antioch was seized by Bohemond, this
leader did not hesitate to repudiate his oath in order to
retain the rich prize. The Christian city of Edessa had
voluntarily called Count Baldwin, the brother of God-
frey of Bouillon, to their aid; but he seized control of it
in a manner reflecting but little credit upon himself.
When Jerusalem fell to the crusaders on July 15, 1099,
a feudal government was set up in what soon became
the kingdom of Jerusalem, which duplicated the feudal
policy and system of the West. The Latin church, of
course, became dominant in the territories conquered
by the Crusaders. The rights of the Greek and the native Christian churches were disregarded. The conquest of the Latins was due not so much to their
strength as to the weakness of the opposing Turkish
forces. When in the end the Turks rallied their forces
and unified their attack under the leadership of Saladin, the Crusaders were decisively defeated at the
Battle of the Horns of Hattin in 1187. This was to all
intents and purposes the end of an effective Christian
rule of Jerusalem.

The calamity which had overtaken the Crusaders
called forth the Third Crusade. This most romantic
expedition was participated in by Emperor Frederick
Barbarossa, King Richard the Lionhearted of England, and his chief foe, King Philip Augustus of
France. The emperor never reached the Holy Land,

having been drowned in a little stream in Asia Minor. Richard conducted some highly chivalric skirmishes with Saladin, although most of the fighting was distinctly unchivalric. In the end the undertaking resulted in a fiasco. Nothing of permanent value was accomplished.

But the most important in the series of Crusades was the Fourth. It was originally intended against Egypt, but the Venetians, upon whom the Crusaders depended for transport, diverted the expedition first against a commercial rival of theirs, the Christian city of Zara, and later against Constantinople. This latter expedition was undertaken in behalf of the dethroned Byzantine emperor, Isaac II. His son, Alexius, had promised the crusading leaders a large sum of money and supplies, military co-operation against the Turks, and the reunion of the Eastern church with the Western. In 1203 the Crusaders succeeded in restoring Isaac to the throne, and his son was crowned as Alexius IV. But both rulers found it impossible to fulfil the promises made to the Crusaders, for their means were insufficient and the people unwilling. In fact, Constantinople rose up in revolt against them and swept them off the throne. Alexius was strangled. Thereupon, the struggle with the Crusaders became inevitable. The latter, early in 1204, decided to attack. After having agreed upon the division of the spoils, of which the Venetians received the lion's share, they captured Constantinople in April, 1204. Thereupon, the enormously rich city was plundered so thoroughly that even the lead of the roofs was ripped off. The

Cathedral of St. Sophia was despoiled and grossly desecrated.

At the time of the conquest the number of Greek clergy and monks was estimated at "a good thirty thousand." Many of the higher clergy, along with Patriarch John X, fled before the Latins, although the vast majority of the lower clergy remained. Despite the fact that it was clearly uncanonical to elect a new patriarch while the rightful occupant of the see was still alive, the Latins created the Venetian, Thomas Morosini, patriarch in 1205. This was an unpropitious beginning for the scheme of Pope Innocent III of securing a reunion between the Eastern and Western churches. No wonder that this undertaking utterly failed. In fact, the hatred engendered by the subjugation and tyranny received by the Greeks at the hands of the Latin conquerors increased enormously and prevented the success of any appeasing or reconciling measures. In the end, the Greek population of Constantinople preferred the Turks to the Latins.

Downfall of the Empire.—The Latin Empire of Rumania, along with the other European feudal states which displaced the Byzantine Empire, was short lived. In 1261 Emperor Michael Palaeologus took Constantinople and re-established the Byzantine dominion. Nevertheless, the Greek Empire never recovered its former strength. Although it survived the blow dealt it by the Fourth Crusade for almost two hundred years, this was due more to negative reasons—namely, the weakness of its Turkish or Christian enemies—rather than to its own positive strength. Michael himself found it necessary to seek help from the West against the threatened invasion of Charles of Anjou, who had inherited the claims to the empire of Rumania. Thus began the desperate and tragic struggle for self-preservation which characterizes the two centuries prior to the downfall of Constantinople. The West demanded an unconditional submission of the Eastern church to the papacy as the price of any aid whatsoever. Michael was driven to make such a submission at the Council of Lyons in 1274, despite the resolute opposition of the Constantinopolitan Patriarch Joseph. Even though the recalcitrant patriarch was deposed and his place taken by a prelate more amenable to the imperial will, the union with Rome was resolutely repudiated by the clergy and the people. In fact, the emperor was afraid to make a public announcement of the union for fear of a violent uprising of his own people. In the end, a catastrophe which overtook the rule of Charles of Anjou in Italy (the so-called Sicilian Vespers of 1282) rendered the threatened invasion of the Byzantine Empire impossible and thus extricated Emperor Michael from a very difficult position. The submission of the Eastern church to the papacy was thus nullified.

But if the empire were freed from the threat of a western invasion, it was confronted with an invasion from the East. The Turks of Asia Minor had long remained unorganized and, consequently, relatively harmless. But the Ottoman Turkish tribe welded the scattered Asia Minor tribes into a strong Turkish state, which then became a real menace to the empire. In

1354 the Turks succeeded in gaining a foothold in Europe by the capture of Gallipoli, whereupon they quickly overran all Thrace. Within a dozen years, the sultan established his capital in the Balkans at Hadrianople and compelled the Byzantine emperor, John V, to sign a treaty which made him practically a Turkish vassal. By 1389, in the fateful Battle of Kosovo Polye, the Turks defeated the union of the Christian Balkan princes and thus became practically the masters of the entire Balkan peninsula. Constantinople was accordingly surrounded on all sides by Turkish-held territories. Its downfall was merely a matter of time. This event was somewhat delayed by the invasion of the Turkish lands by Timur, which gave the Byzantine Empire a short respite. Realizing that without western aid the fall of Constantinople was inevitable, Emperor John VIII made one more attempt to secure aid from the western Christians. He appealed both to Pope Eugenius IV and to the Council of Basel, which was then meeting. The pope utilized this opportunity to monopolize the negotiations with the Eastern church and thus to secure for himself the credit for the victory. After long negotiations with the emperor and the representatives of the Greek church carried on at the Council of Florence, the Greeks were finally compelled to yield to the demands of the Roman church all along the line. This, then, led to the famous Union of Florence, proclaimed in 1439.

But when Emperor John returned to Constantinople, he encountered the same opposition which had met Emperor Michael VIII in 1274. The mass of

Greek clergy and the people utterly repudiated the Florentine Union. Had the western military aid been quickly organized and sent east, John might have been enabled to impose the union upon his unwilling subjects; but the western leaders were dilatory and disunited. Emperor John died in 1448 and was succeeded by his brother, Constantine XI, who was opposed to the union, and, moreover, this measure was repudiated by a council in 1450. Under these circumstances, the East was once more constrained to face the Turkish menace without an adequate western support.

It was in 1453 that the Turkish sultan, Mohammed II, made up his mind to take Constantinople. He attacked it from the sea, but the city defended itself valiantly; in the end, however, a brilliant stratagem brought the sultan victory. The Byzantine Empire ceased to exist on May 29, 1453.

Effect upon the church.—The downfall of the Byzantine Empire did not destroy the Byzantine church. It survived and, in fact, absorbed some of the powers formerly exercised by the imperial government. The sultan appointed a new patriarch, Gennadius II, and himself invested him with the scepter of office. Moreover, he confirmed the patriarch and his clergy in their former privileges and exempted them from all taxes. But besides the ecclesiastical rule exercised by the patriarch over the Christians under his jurisdiction, he also was intrusted with functions which were of political character. The patriarch became the "ethnarch, lord, and emperor" of all Christian Greeks within the Turkish sultanate. They were formed into a separate community (*Rum milet*) which was not subject to the Turkish law and courts. Since the Moslems regarded the Koran as their only lawbook, both civil and religious, the Christians could not be subjected to it. Thus the Christian community was governed by its own patriarch on the basis of the old Byzantine laws. Accordingly, the patriarch became the head of the Greek community within the Turkish Empire in matters both civil and ecclesiastical. It is for this reason that the sultan regarded the appointment of the patriarch as of great political importance, and it was this feature that ultimately led to a great deal of interference on his part in the appointment of the candidates for that office.

Had these mild and on the whole favorable conditions established by Mohammed II been observed by the Turkish sultans, the lot of the conquered Christians would have been vastly different from the one which actually prevailed. But, unfortunately, even Mohammed himself did not always observe the provisions of his own making. The taxation grew exceedingly heavy, and the corruptions of the system made it even more burdensome than the tax itself. It was particularly the so-called "blood tax," that is, the forcible recruiting of the most favored children of Christian parents for training in the famous Turkish regiment of the "Yanisari" and for governmental posts, which proved exceedingly galling. Moreover, the patriarchal office, by reason of its great political power, became the goal of many unworthy schemers who seized it by bribery, until this method was hardened into a regular system. All these causes resulted in the degradation of the Greek population within the Turkish dominion to an exploited, oppressed class of raias, or virtual slavery. The centuries-long subjection to these degrading conditions resulted in incalculable damage to the spiritual power and influence of the Christian churches within the Turkish dominions.

19. THE RUSSIAN CHURCH TO THE REVOLUTION OF 1917

The Russian church under Byzantine control.—As has been mentioned previously, Russia was converted to Christianity in the reign of Grand Prince Vladimir in 987. Christianity had existed in Russia previous to the reign of this prince. In fact, he had been brought up in Christian nurture by his Christian grandmother, Olga. Moreover, the Scandinavian community of Kiev, the capital of the principality and at present the chief city of the Ukraine, comprised some Christians, for they possessed a church of St. Elijah which is mentioned in the middle of the tenth century. Nevertheless, Vladimir's conversion marks the official adoption of Christianity by the prince who, in turn, imposed it upon the nation. By the time of the prince's death, in 1015, Christianity may be said to have been introduced into most of the country. To be sure, the work of Christianization was slow and imperfect, but it continued to make progress. The higher clergy, together with the head of the Russian church, the metropolitan, were Greeks sent to Russia from Constantinople. However, the lower clergy were either trained in native schools or were secured from Bulgaria. The Slavic version of the Scriptures and of the liturgical books was also taken over from Bulgaria.

The progress of Christianity in Russia was fairly satisfactory. Moreover, the native element slowly made itself felt against the power of the higher Greek clergy. Undoubtedly, had Russian Christianity been allowed to develop uninterrupted, it would have produced a relatively high type of culture. But this was not to be its fate.

Early in the thirteenth century the Mongols first found their way into southern Russia. It appears that they came quite unintentionally, possibly by chance. Nevertheless, this fortuitous discovery of the rich lands of the Russians and of their capital, Kiev, led to a later invasion which was definitely planned. This occurred in 1237, when the Tartars invaded Russia again under the leadership of Batu. He succeeded, by 1240, in conquering Kiev and mastering the whole territory.

The defeated Russians sought escape by flight. One group of refugees fled to Galicia, which at present forms the southern part of Poland. Another mass of refugees fled in a northeastern direction and settled the territory which later came to be known as the grand principality of Moscow. Thus Kiev ceased to be the Russian capital, and there now existed two main Russian principalities, the Galician and the Great Russian.

The metropolitan of the Russian church was in the habit of visiting these two widely divided groups subject to his jurisdiction and spending a part of the year with each of them. It was his decision to settle permanently at Moscow which gave pre-eminence to this hitherto insignificant hamlet. This change was made by Metropolitan Peter, who thus laid the foundation of the later political pre-eminence of Moscow over the other Russian principalities.

Nevertheless, the Russian church continued to live under the supreme jurisdiction of the patriarch of Constantinople. This dependence upon the Byzantine church came to an end only shortly before the downfall of the Byzantine Empire. As has already been narrated, the Byzantine Empire was driven to accept the so-called Florentine Union, negotiated in 1439. The Russian metropolitan, a Greek by the name of Isidore, not only approved the union with Rome but even played the chief role in the negotiations. But when he attempted to read the act of Florentine Union in the Cathedral of the Assumption in the Kremlin of Moscow, Grand Prince Vasily violently interrupted him and forbade the reading. Moreover, he ordered Isidore to be imprisoned and tried. But the Russian church council had no canonical authority to depose the metropolitan without the consent of the patriarch of Constantinople. Vasily found himself in a difficult situation. In the end, he allowed Isidore to escape from prison and to run away from Russia. After an interregnum, Vasily ordered the Russian episcopate to consecrate one of their number as the new metropolitan (1448). The choice fell on Bishop Jonah, and his consecration by the local Russian council signifies the end of the Constantinopolitan jurisdiction over the Russian church.

Patriarchate of Russia.—The Byzantine Empire fell in 1453. Thereafter, the Byzantine church was subject to the Turkish power. In the course of time, Russia came to feel that their grand prince became the heir of the Byzantine imperial dignity and that the church inherited the primacy among the Eastern Orthodox churches. Grand Prince John III, having married Sophia Palaeologa, the niece of the last Byzantine emperor, was the first to assume the title of Caesar, that is, Czar, and to adopt the Byzantine two-headed eagle as his imperial emblem. The church signified a similar assumption of leadership of Eastern Orthodoxy by adopting the theory that Moscow is the "third Rome." They maintained that originally Rome had been at the head of Christendom, and that later Constantinople had secured the headship, but because of the latter's betrayal of Orthodoxy in the Florentine Union, the hegemony had passed to Moscow.

This increase of self-consciousness and assumption of leadership and headship were inconsistent with the inferior rank which the metropolitan of Moscow held. After all, the Greeks could boast of four patriarchs, despite their insignificant dioceses. Accordingly, the final step in the rise to power and dominant influence of the Russian church came with the conferring of the patriarchal dignity upon the metropolitan of Moscow. This occurred in 1589, when the ecumenical patriarch, Jeremiah II, visited Russia in quest of financial aid. He was practically forced to grant the czar's request for the patriarchal rank for the Russian church before he received the desired gift and was permitted to leave

Russia. In this way, then, the Russian church at last became an independent national church of patriarchal rank.

The patriarchate soon was subjected to a severe test during the so-called "troubled times" which overtook Russia after the death of the weak-witted czar Feodor. The latter died in 1598, and with him expired the last scion of the House of Rurik.

It was not until 1613 that the council elected the sixteen-year-old Michael Feodorovich Romanov to the throne. His father, who had become a monk and had assumed the name of Philaret, became patriarch of Russia in 1619. Thus Russia was governed by son and father.

During the reign of Czar Michael Russia became accustomed to regarding the czar and patriarch as of almost equal authority in their two respective spheres. Thus the office of patriarch was greatly raised in dignity.

The most outstanding of the successors of Philaret was Patriarch Nikon. This very able and forceful man of humble origins was chosen by Czar Alexius Michaelovich, who made him his close friend and adviser. But the great power wielded by the patriarch was resented by the nobles of the czar's court who plotted to estrange the czar from the patriarch. This was accomplished by a campaign of defamation which was not difficult to conduct, since the patriarch was far more forthright than tactful. The situation was complicated by a reform conducted by the patriarch but resented by the masses. This was the correction of the Russian liturgical service-books and other literature which

Nikon decided must be brought into conformity with the Greek text. Many churchmen regarded this as a slur on the sanctity of the Russian church and as a concession to the hated Greeks, who were looked upon as heretical in tendency. This embroilment was utilized by the enemies of the patriarch to plot his downfall. They succeeded in poisoning the czar's mind against his former friend. Patriarch Nikon on the whole defended the policy of the independence of the church in matters spiritual and the harmony of the ecclesiastical and the civil spheres. The opposing group advocated the theory that the state is superior to the church. In the end, Patriarch Nikon was deposed from his office in 1667. This was done on the authority of two eastern patriarchs, who came to Moscow for the trial. Nevertheless, the council approved Nikon's church reform and pronounced a curse upon all who would refuse to submit to it.

This decision resulted in the so-called Great Schism of 1666, for a large group within the church—the Old Believers—refused to submit to the Nikonian reforms. The schism persists to this day.

Church subjected to the state.—The defeat of Patriarch Nikon represented the victory of the secular government over the church. The process was completed in the days of Peter the Great. Before he assumed the rule, Peter had traveled in Europe, particularly in Holland and England, where he had absorbed many ideas which he later strove to realize in Russia. With him, therefore, begins the so-called westernization of Russia.

As far as the church was concerned, the czar, who was irreligious, used it only to further his political and cultural designs. When Patriarch Adrian died in 1700, Peter refused to allow a successor to be nominated or elected. In this way the Russian patriarchate came to an end.

In 1721 Peter instituted a new order into the Russian church. He set up the so-called "Holy Governing Synod," which in course of time became a governmental department for the control of the church. Members of the synod were appointed by the czar and were supervised by his personal representative, a layman, who received the title of Ober-Procuror. It was in this way that the ancient liberties of the Russian church were completely subverted. But it must be noted, in justice to the Russian church, that the latter was the victim of this aggressive measure rather than a free agent voluntarily subjecting itself to the power of the state.

The story of the Russian church from now on is a sad and tragic one. The organization was utilized more and more for political purposes, although the spiritual life of the church survived even under these circumstances. There is no need to describe in detail the gradual degradation of the church; it will be more profitable to consider the astonishingly virile movement of revival which arose in the nineteenth century and which is the best proof that the Russian church is not to be identified merely with the ecclesiastical and hierarchical organization subservient to the autocratic Russian czarism.

Nineteenth-century Russia was divided culturally into two dominant parties: the Westernists and the Slavophils. Most of the great names in literature belong to the former group. These leaders pursued the ideal of making Russia culturally one with western Europe. Politically, they opposed the czarist autocracy and worked for a limited monarchy or some other form of relatively liberal government. Philosophically, most of them were materialists or positivists, and religiously many of them were out-and-out atheists. The Slavophils, on the other hand, believed that there were valuable elements in the Russian native culture and strove to bring these to fruition. Since Russian Orthodoxy was part and parcel of the native culture, they became exponents and interpreters of it. Accordingly, this party produced most of the leaders of the modern Russian religio-philosophical movements. The novelist, Dostoyevsky, is the best known of the group, because his works are available in English. His unfinished novel, *Brothers Karamazov*, is the best popular exposition of the religious philosophy of this group. His opposition to westernism was based upon his perception of the destructive forces, political and economic, as well as individual and social, inherent in this view of life. His insight was almost uncanny. The fate of modern Soviet Russia, and in fact of most of Europe, testifies to the truth of his analysis of the destructive forces inherent in the "westernist" cultural world-view. The most distinguished of the modern representatives of this school is N. Berdyaev, whose writings exercise great influence upon the present theological thinking of Europe and America.

20. THE POST-WAR EASTERN ORTHODOX CHURCHES

The Russian churches.—With the downfall of the Russian Empire in 1917, the fate of the Russian Orthodox church—in fact, of Russian organized religion—was sealed. The victorious Bolshevist party had long ago adopted atheism as an integral part of its world-view. Accordingly, the struggle against the Russian church was not waged for the purpose of reforming or purifying this church but because the destruction of all religion was one of the primary tenets of the Marxian ideology. According to Marx's theory, the capitalistic order of society is founded upon religious bases; consequently, religion must be destroyed before the capitalistic superstructure can be overthrown.

The first laws regarding religion were issued in January, 1918. As far as the letter of the law went, this code granted liberty of confession and practice—under certain strict regulations—to all. The intention and execution of the law, however, aimed at the destruction of the church. The church lost all its property—churches, schools lands, and other assets—and, of course, the governmental subsidy as well. Thus, the church was left without means of support, save the voluntary aid of the faithful. But a more serious threat to its life was the prohibition of religious instruction in all schools, which now passed under the control of the government. All public religious instruction of children under eighteen years of age was forbidden. Moreover, the clergy were deprived of rights of franchise as well as of other rights. These deprivations seriously affected their economic status and their possibility of earning a living.

The attempt on the part of Patriarch Tikhon, who was elected in 1917, when the patriarchate was restored, to defy the destructive policy of the state led to the division of the church into two chief parties—the Living Church, later transformed into the Synodical party, and the Patriarchal party. Tikhon himself was imprisoned. The former group acknowledged the Soviet government and submitted to its political authority. The Patriarchal party was subjected to rigorous repressive measures. After the death of Patriarch Tikhon (1925), the convening of a council for the election of his successor was forbidden. Since then the party has been without a patriarch and is headed by a "keeper of the patriarchal throne." To all intents and purposes, it has been so broken and subjected to the dictates of the government that its present strength is negligible. The Synodical party had received a certain amount of support from the government on the theory of "divide and rule," but there is no fundamental difference in the fate of these two groups.

The situation was radically changed in 1929 with the inauguration of the Five-Year Plan. The cultural policy of this plan aimed at indoctrination of the populace in communism. The religious liberties hitherto existing were accordingly abolished. The constitution of most of the Soviet republics was changed in such a way that "liberty of religious confession" was indeed reiterated, but the right of "propaganda" was denied. Thus "liberty of conscience" amounts to no more than the privilege of holding a bare religious service. Accordingly, religious freedom in any real sense no longer exists.

At the same time, antireligious propaganda of great effectiveness, supported by all the resources of the government, was launched. It invaded all schools, press, and the radio; it was supplemented by economic pressure in order to win its objectives. Congregations of believers were taxed so heavily that they had to disband "voluntarily." Almost as many churches were closed during the first year of this period as throughout the entire previous period.

As a consequence of this merciless and persistent attack upon the church, all organized ecclesiastical life has been practically destroyed. Of course, that does not mean that Russian Christianity is nonexistent; but it has been driven underground. If persecutions on a large scale have ceased, it is because the leaders of the antireligious propaganda are convinced that the task has been accomplished and that "there is no use flogging a dead horse."

The Greek group and the patriarchates.—Let us pass now to the Greek group of Orthodox churches which consists of the patriarchate of Constantinople, the national church of Greece, the Greek church of the Dodecanese Islands, of Crete, and the patriarchate of Alexandria. The patriarchate of Constantinople, the lineal descendant of the imperial Byzantine church, suffered more disastrous changes after the war of 1914–18 than when the Turks had conquered Constantinople in 1453. The new Republic of Turkey, under Mustapha Kemal Pasha, determined to expel the ecumenical patriarchate from the Turkish territories altogether. Restrained from this radical step by the British diplomacy at the Lausanne Conference in 1923, the Turks at least deposed Patriarch Meletios and deprived the patriarchate of all but spiritual power over the Greek Christians within Turkey.

Moreover, the plan of forcible exchange of population resulted in all but the total ruin of Christianity within Turkey. With the exception of the Greeks established in Istanbul and its vicinity prior to October, 1918, all the rest of the Christian population of Turkey had to leave the country. Some one and a half millions emigrated from Asia Minor and Thrace and found new homes mostly in Greece. Only four metropolitanates out of forty-one survived this catastrophe, some of the ruined sees having been among the most ancient and celebrated, with traditions which went back to the times of the apostle Paul. Thus one of the countries in which ancient Christianity had its earliest successes, Asia Minor, has been lost to Christianity in our own times.

The Church of the Republic of Greece goes back for its beginnings in modern times to the year 1833. The Greeks secured ecclesiastical independence from the ecumenical patriarchate by the middle of the nineteenth century. But as has been all too often the case with Eastern Orthodox communions, the church fell under the sway of the state. This situation was well

illustrated during the war of 1914–18, when the archiepiscopal see of Athens changed occupants with almost every political change.

In 1923, as a result of the forcible exchange of population, the membership in the Church of Greece was
enormously swelled by the influx of one and a half
million Greeks from Asia Minor and Thrace. The task
of absorbing this large number of new arrivals for a
time greatly taxed the strength of the state as well as
the church.

At the present time, the dictatorial regime of General Metaxas has inaugurated a phase of nationalistic
opposition to foreign influence which manifests itself in
a sweeping restriction of missionary work. But in effect
this is directed against the Roman Catholic missions,
suspected of Italian political orientation, far more than
against Protestant work.

There are three other Greek churches in the Near
East: the Orthodox church of Cyprus, which was
granted independence in 431; the Church of the
Dodecanese Islands, which since the conclusion of the
war of 1914–18 has been controlled by the Italians;
and the patriarchate of Alexandria, the membership of
which is about two-thirds Greek.

The patriarchate of Jerusalem, at one time the
mother-church of Christendom, comprises some forty
thousand members, almost all of whom are Arabs.
But the control is concentrated in the hands of Greeks,
members of the Brotherhood of the Holy Sepulcher,
numbering a mere handful. A fierce struggle is being
waged by the native population for the wresting of the

control from the Greeks, which reflects the upsurge of the Arab national consciousness throughout the Arab world.

A similar struggle for the control of the church had been waged some forty years previously by the patriarchate of Antioch. This Syriac church had been controlled by a small group of Greeks. But in 1899 this foreign domination was overthrown by the election of a native patriarch. Since then the see of Antioch has continued as a purely native church.

The Balkan group and the newer churches.—The Balkan group of Orthodox communions, by reason of the tragic fate which had overtaken the Russian church, has become the most numerous and the most important in the entire confraternity of Eastern churches. The largest of the Balkan units was the Rumanian church. Rumania had more than doubled its territory after the war of 1914–18; as a result, it consolidated several formerly separate church bodies into one national Orthodox church. The unified body then boasted of some thirteen million members. The Rumanian Orthodox church is designated in the constitution as "dominant in the state"; the church next in numerical strength, the Uniate (a church originally Orthodox, which submitted to the supreme jurisdiction of the Roman pope), was granted the status of "priority among the cults." The unprecedented rise to power and influence led to the establishment of the Rumanian patriarchate—a rank which the church never before possessed.

A similar expansion of territory and consequent accession of power and dignity was experienced by the Serbian church. With the unification of the Serbians, Croatians, and Slovenes, the population of the new unified kingdom religiously comprised almost as many Roman Catholics as Serbian Orthodox.

As for the Serbian Orthodox church, it is the result of unification of six formerly separate units. The consolidation was accomplished in 1920, and at the same time the new church resumed the patriarchal rank which it had formerly possessed.

Bulgaria is likewise an Orthodox country. In fact, the independence of the church from the control of the patriarchate of Constantinople preceded the political freedom of the state from the rule of the Turks. The struggle over ecclesiastical independence, which succeeded in 1872, produced an estrangement from the ecumenical patriarchate and other Greek churches which has persisted to this day.

The last and youngest of the Balkan Orthodox churches is that of Albania, which freed itself from the control of the ecumenical patriarchate only after the war of 1914–18.

Besides these churches, most of which are of ancient foundations, there is a group of younger churches, many of which owe their origin to favorable conditions consequent upon the war of 1914–18. Such, for instance, are the Orthodox churches of Czechoslovakia, Poland, Finland, Estonia, and Lithuania. When Czechoslovakia was in the process of formation, the Ruthenians asked to be included in the new state, for they did not wish to remain within Hungary, nor did they desire to enter the Soviet Union or Poland. These people, originally Orthodox, had been constrained to accept Uniatism. But when they received religious liberty in Czechoslovakia, they promptly returned. The Orthodox church of Finland is likely to disappear, for the territory which it occupied in the southeast lately reverted to Russia. The new political alignment of many of these countries will undoubtedly produce radical changes in their ecclesiastical status.

Separated communions.—Besides the Eastern Orthodox communions, there still exists in the Near East a number of ancient churches which for various reasons find themselves separated and hence outside the confederation of the Orthodox group. They are the churches of Egypt (the Coptic), of Ethiopia, the National Syrian church (Jacobite), the Assyrian (Nestorian), and the Armenian.

Such, then, in brief, is the story of Eastern Christianity, the third component part of the Church Ecumenical.

CHAPTER VI

CHRISTIANITY IN MODERN EUROPE

21. AFTERMATH OF THE REFORMATION

Cross-section of Europe in 1600.—By the end of the sixteenth century Protestantism was firmly established as the official religion in the north German states, the western cantons of Switzerland, the Dutch republic, England, Scotland, and the Scandinavian countries. After a generation of religious wars, the Protestants in France (Huguenots) had gained freedom of worship in certain limited areas under the Edict of Nantes (1598), which gave them, as a guaranty of their liberties, certain political and military privileges that made them almost a state within a state. Strong Protestant parties had developed in Poland and Hungary, where considerations of political expediency had given religious liberty for a time; but dynastic changes made possible the renewal of persecution, urged by the Jesuits, and the Protestant following was virtually destroyed in Poland and was greatly reduced in Hungary.

After its first rapid expansion and the losses just mentioned, the advancing wave of Protestantism had come to a standstill. Catholic and Protestant forces were in equilibrium. Each party had entrenched itself in the area that it possessed with little prospect of making substantial inroads on the other. The religious map of western Europe in 1600 was not very different from a map drawn for the present day.

Since Roman Catholicism had always utilized the power of the state for the suppression of heretics and dissenters, and was continuing to do so wherever it could, Protestantism adopted the same method to win and hold its ground. Alliance between church and state and the theory that a state must have a single authorized religion protected by the state from the competition of other faiths were features of medieval Catholicism which were carried over into Protestantism. Only such marginal and irregular groups as the Anabaptists (and later the Independents, Baptists, and Quakers) considered religion a matter for free individual choice and disavowed the right of the state either to interfere with it or to gain adherents to it by the exercise of the police power. Europe consisted of a number of Catholic powers and a number of Protestant powers, each granting only a limited amount of tolerance to the opposite faith. Catholic Spain granted no religious liberty; Protestant Netherlands granted a great deal. The policies of Protestant England and Catholic France varied according to political pressures. In England, by 1600, the reign of Queen Elizabeth, who had treated Catholics as traitors because the pope had deposed her and released her subjects from their allegiance, was nearing its end; while in France the reign of Henry IV, who, having previously been a Protestant, had given a degree of liberty to Protestants in order to end the civil strife with a powerful minority which apparently could not be crushed, was just at its beginning. Developments during the seventeenth century brought more liberty to Catholics in England and less to Protestants in France.

The seventeenth century dawned upon a Roman Catholicism strengthened by the removal of many of its most scandalous abuses, by the restatement of its position in the decrees of the Council of Trent, and by the formation of many new religious orders. Of these latter, the Jesuits were the most militant and the most serviceable. Though they were already the objects of general suspicion by Catholic governments, by the regular clergy, and by other religious orders, they had given proof of their efficiency in missionary work in the Far East, in the beginning of educational work which was to grow to vast dimensions, and in winning back some areas, such as Poland, which had been deeply invaded by the Reformation.

Protestantism, on the other hand, was weakened by its divisions. One must not think of Protestantism as originally a united movement which later divided. It was a number of independent movements which struggled toward a unity that they never attained. The more important Protestant bodies came into existence as territorial or national churches. There might be co-operation or conference among them, as there sometimes was, but each was independent of the others, and they had no common plan of action. There were also theological differences. To the Lutheran, Calvinistic, and Socinian systems were soon to be added the Arminian and the Anglican.

Religious struggles of the seventeenth century.—The seventeenth century has been called "that wretched century of strife." Of course, there was more to it than that. But the Thirty Years' War in Germany, the violent suppression of Protestantism in France, and the Civil War in England were enough to justify the phrase.

The Thirty Years' War (1618–48) began as a religious conflict in Bohemia and Germany, but it became a general European war, drawing into itself all other wars of the time. The Catholic hierarchy and princes were alarmed by the rapid progress that Lutheranism had made after the Peace of Augsburg (1555) had given it legal standing in the Empire. The Protestant states were alarmed by the vigorous efforts of the Catholic church to regain lost ground and by its disposition to consider the Peace of Augsburg as a mere interim arrangement that could be disregarded wherever and whenever political conditions and military power permitted. Following the capture of the free and Protestant city of Donauwörth by the (Catholic) Holy League, a Protestant union was organized. Still the opposing forces were held in check until the election of a Calvinist as king of Bohemia roused the Catholic forces of the Empire to battle for the extirpation of heresy.

Most of the fighting was on German soil. Few wars in history have been more destructive and devastating. Every nationalistic and dynastic ambition in Europe became involved in the Thirty Years' War, and many of its leaders had little interest in religion. It was by no means a clear-cut contest between Catholics and Protestants. But the religious issue furnished the original stimulus and played an important part both in the alignment of forces and in the Peace of Westphalia, which ended the war. The great Protestant champion was Gustavus Adolphus, king of Sweden. By the terms of the peace, each state within the Empire was to have the religion of its prince, whether Catholic, Lutheran, or Calvinistic. (The Peace of Augsburg had allowed a choice only between Catholicism and Lutheranism.) The principle of religious solidarity of states was thus reaffirmed. The only religious liberty guaranteed was the right of a citizen to emigrate if he could not conform to the religion of his prince. But populations had been so decimated by the war and man-power was so much needed for the rebuilding of what had been destroyed that, in practice, most of the princes (except some who were also Catholic prelates) preferred to be more tolerant than the treaty required rather than lose citizens from their depleted states. The pope issued a bull denouncing the treaty and declaring null and void all parts of it which professed to settle religious matters, because "the heretics, called those of the Augsburg Confession, are permitted the free exercise of their heresy in various districts and are admitted with Catholics to public offices and positions." But his protest was ignored even by the Catholic princes.

Soon after Henry IV became king of France he gave the Protestants a charter of rights called the Edict of Nantes (1598). In spite of the efforts to exterminate it in the sixteenth century, Protestantism in the form taught by Calvin had become the religion of something more than one-tenth of the people of France, but their industry, wealth, and intelligence gave them an importance out of proportion to their numbers. Relatively few of them were peasants, and many were prosperous tradesmen and skilled craftsmen in the towns. Henry IV was assassinated in 1610, and soon there began a new campaign against the Huguenots; first, to take away the military power which Henry had, perhaps unwisely, given them; and then to wipe them out. The first part of this program was successfully carried out by Cardinal Richelieu, who was Louis XIII's prime minister. When they had been rendered helpless by disarming them and taking away their control of the towns in which they had their strength, a policy of terrorism which forced conversion to Catholicism was adopted, culminating in the revocation of the Edict of Nantes by Louis XIV in 1685. The king pretended, and perhaps was led to believe, that there were no more Protestants in France. This was far from the truth, for, even after something like four hundred thousand had emigrated to other countries, still more remained to become the object of renewed persecutions.

Dutch and English Protestantism.—The northern half of the Netherlands had become Protestant early in the sixteenth century and had won independence from Spain by the end of that century, though Spain did not acknowledge it until the Peace of Westphalia (1648). The southern part, which was to become Belgium, remained Catholic and did not gain its independence until much later. The Protestant Netherlands, strongly Calvinistic, became involved for a time in a theologi-

cal struggle, almost as fierce as the wars for liberation
had been. The teachings of a professor named James
Arminius were championed at the Synod of Dort
(1618) by a party who called themselves Remonstrants. They were condemned and banned for rejecting the doctrine of predestination. Arminianism became the most important deviation from the strict
Calvinistic theory of immutable divine decrees determining from all eternity whether each man is to be
saved or lost. Arminianism taught that God exercises
his sovereignty in such a way as to leave man free to
accept or to reject his grace. It strongly influenced the
Church of England and (later) the Methodist movement. Except for a brief persecution of the Armin-
ians, the Netherlands became and long remained the
country which granted wider religious liberty than any
other in Europe. Early English Independents (Congregationalists), including our Pilgrim Fathers, sought
refuge in the Netherlands when they were persecuted
in England.

The Reformation in England had, from the first, assumed that there was to be a national church and that
the king was to be its head. But when James I came
to the throne (1603), it was not yet clear just what kind
of church the Church of England was to be. It had
bishops and a liturgical service set forth in a prayer-
book, and its ministers wore priestly vestments. But
there was a large Puritan (or Presbyterian) element in
the church who were opposed to all these things.
Scotland had become thoroughly Presbyterian, largely
through the influence of John Knox. So when James,

who was already king of Scotland, became also king of England, it remained to be seen whether the Presbyterian element in the Church of England would prevail. It did not. Through all the turmoil of that stormy century—the downfall of royal absolutism, the beheading of Charles I, the Civil War, the Commonwealth under Cromwell, the restoration of the monarchy under Charles II, the deposition of James II, and the complete end of royal absolutism with the crowning of William and Mary—there was a series of religious developments which gave the Church of England and the dissenting bodies something like their present status.

Episcopacy, which had been held as a good working system consistent with the principle of monarchy (so Hooker had defended it in his *Ecclesiastical Polity*), now began to be reinforced by the doctrine, new to Protestant England, that divine authority required the church to have bishops who are in unbroken succession from the Apostles. Archbishop Laud became the outstanding spokesman for this position. The Presbyterians were equally sure that their system of polity was divinely commanded. Between these two views there could be no compromise, and the two could not be included within one church. After a brief period of Puritan predominance during the Commonwealth, the Restoration made the Church of England definitely episcopalian. Puritans, including not only Presbyterians but also Independents and Baptists, who had gained considerable numbers, were forced out of the church. Under the Act of Uniformity Puritan ministers were treated as criminals. The severity of this repression gradually diminished, and in 1689 an Act of Toleration gave freedom of worship to all dissenters, though they were still under some civil disabilities. Within the century the Church of England had become a definitely homogeneous episcopal denomination, but while it continued to be the national church, headed by the king and enjoying special favors from the state, it had ceased to be the church of the whole nation by excluding from itself large bodies of nonconformists.

22. ADVENTURES IN FAITH AND FREEDOM
(ABSOLUTISM AND DEMOCRACY)

While science, philosophy, literature, industry, and religion (in some of its phases) were promoting the development of the democratic spirit and were furnishing fields for the exercise of the freedom of the individual, political absolutism was building up toward the inevitable revolution. In tracing the history of religion it will be necessary for us to observe some of the ways in which men were discovering and asserting the worth and the rights of man. In so far as religion hindered the attainment of liberty, as it sometimes did, it forfeited the loyalty of important groups of people, some of whom are now honored as leaders in human progress and most of whom would have been ardent supporters of a religion that was on the side of human rights. But we must see all these liberating movements against a background of arbitrary rule imposed by most of the sovereigns and repressive authoritarianism practiced by most of the churches.

In England the "bloodless revolution" of 1688 put an end to the futile efforts of the Stuart kings to make the royal power absolute. England was a century ahead of the Continental countries in this respect. In France royal absolutism reached its highest glory under Louis XIV (1643–1715), but its theory and its pretensions continued until the French Revolution brought it to a tragic conclusion with the execution of Louis XVI. Spain and the dominions of the emperor made no concessions to popular rights or the consent of the governed. The sovereigns of the many independent states in Germany and Italy not only reigned but ruled. The Papal State, which still occupied all central Italy, was the most absolute monarchy of all. The eighteenth century is sometimes called "the Age of Reason," sometimes "the Age of Benevolent Despots." Not all the despots were benevolent, but there were many princes—such as Frederick the Great (1740–86), who found Prussia a small power and left it a great one, and Holy Roman Emperor Joseph II (1765–90), who tried to introduce religious liberty and social reform by royal edict—who were favorable to every form of intellectual freedom and friendly to all liberal ideas outside the field of government. Frederick was nominally a Protestant but really indifferent to religion; Joseph, a Catholic, came near to breaking with the church, which opposed and frustrated his reforms.

Nowhere were the established churches wholly on the side of liberty, yet they performed a service by opposing a secular totalitarianism. The Roman Catholic church, claiming itself to be the final arbiter of public as well as private affairs, brought strong pressure to bear upon Catholic sovereigns whose arbitrary policies seemed to endanger its interests; and Catholic writers, like Suarez and Bellarmine, sought to reduce the independence of the sovereigns by showing that their power (unlike that of the church) was derived from the people by a social contract. Protestant state churches, carrying over from Catholicism the idea of compulsory religious uniformity, fell far short of granting the individual liberty which was implicit in their basic principles. They tended to become subordinate to the state. In the German states this meant, according to the Peace of Westphalia, that the people were required to profess the religion of the ruler. In England, however, especially after 1689, it meant that the ruler must profess the religion approved by Parliament.

In practice, the Protestant countries tended toward toleration both for dissenting forms of religion and for scientific and philosophical thought which some considered subversive of the faith. The tradition of free speech and "unlicensed printing" became established in England and the Netherlands in the seventeenth century. The Protestant Reformation, especially in its early stages, had stressed the worth and dignity of the individual, the ability of every man to approach God without the mediation of a priest, and the right of

every man to interpret divine revelation without defer-
ence to the authority of the church and its tradition.
After the first crystallization of Protestantism into in-
tolerant state churches, there came a reassertion of this
implicit individualism, limited as it was by an equal
insistence that the "priesthood of believers" could be
fully exercised only within the fellowship of a Christian
community. Furthermore, the suppression of large minorities was found to be politically inexpedient as well
as morally odious. Thus England got a toleration act
in 1689 which gave religious liberty (though not yet
full civil rights) to dissenters; the Protestant Netherlands became a refuge for the persecuted from other
countries; and the Protestant German states, whether
Lutheran or Calvinistic, ceased to penalize the adherents of the other faith. All this made for the progress of civil liberty, for freedom of thought and expression, and for the development of the democratic spirit.

Tolerance and the Age of Reason.—In France, the foremost country on the Continent in the eighteenth century, the alliance of the monarchy with the Catholic
church prevented the growth of religious liberty.
Protestantism, again officially pronounced extinct by
Louis XIV in 1715, five months before his own death
—and thirty years after he had justified his revocation
of the Edict of Nantes by the same statement—organized the first synod of "the Church in the Desert."
Its services were celebrated in secret, and its members
were without civil rights. Because marriages at which
its ministers officiated were deemed void, Protestants
were all legally illegitimate. The development of secu-

lar humanitarianism and free thought among the people, and the detachment of the intellectual classes from the authority of the church by the influence of such "free-thinkers" as Montesquieu, Rousseau, and Voltaire, built up popular sentiment favoring religious liberty. It was not until 1787, however, two years before the Revolution, that the civil rights of Protestants were partially restored by recognizing their marriages as valid—against the fierce protests of the Catholic clergy. A Protestant pastor, son of the second head of the Synod of the Desert, was a deputy in the States-General of 1789. He declared: "It is not tolerance which I demand; it is liberty." But it had taken the explosion of the French Revolution to get it.

While the churches had been deeply involved in struggles for dominance or for liberty, there had risen a large class of people who had little interest in religion. Some of these were statesmen for whom churches were pawns in the political game. Some were poets and dramatists who, though not necessarily antireligious, were concerned with purely secular topics and appealed to a public in whose minds secular interests had first place. In the Middle Ages most writers were priests or monks and most literature was religious. The Renaissance of the fifteenth century produced many lay writers (or priestly writers who wrote like laymen) and much secular literature. That tendency continued and increased more rapidly in the seventeenth and eighteenth centuries. Besides these popular authors there was a notable succession of philosophers and scientists who assumed the right of free thought and free research. Some of these were churchmen whose churchmanship was only incidental, like Copernicus, who was cautious enough to escape interference from the authorities, and Giordano Bruno, who, being less cautious, and living in an age in which the church had become more sensitive to the dangers of free thought, was burned by the Inquisition at Rome. Most of them were laymen. Such, for example, were Descartes, a French Catholic; John Locke, an English Protestant; Leibnitz, a German Protestant; and Spinoza, a Spanish Jew (by descent) who lived in the Netherlands.

The important thing is that there rose a large class of intellectual leaders who, as independent laymen, sought for truth without asking aid from the theologians and without permitting restraint from the ecclesiastics, and that these leaders found a large audience of readers and followers. This was nothing less than an intellectual revolution. In the long run it profoundly affected the course of religious thought and the attitudes of the intelligent classes toward religion.

By the eighteenth century the spirit of scientific inquiry based on the observation of facts and free philosophical thought based either upon experience (empiricism) or upon the processes of human reason (rationalism) had become so widespread that the period is appropriately called the Age of Reason. Its fundamental idea was that the individual man has the ability to find the truth by the use of his senses and his reason and the right to do so and to announce his conclusions. Authority and revelation were discounted if not repudiated. This became the attitude not only of the intellectual leaders but of a large proportion of the political leaders and of the middle class.

The characteristics of the "middle class" had been greatly altered by developments of industry and trade which began to give business much of its modern form. It would be an exaggeration to say that capitalism and the middle class came into existence after the Reformation, but they rose to new importance and took on a different character. With the decay of feudalism, new forms of both wealth and poverty appeared. Doubtless free thought in philosophy and free investigation in science were matters of small concern either to most of the new-rich, who were profiting by colonial trade and factory production, or to the new-poor, who suffered from agricultural depression and industrial exploitation; but both realized that they were involved, for better or worse, in an economic system in which religion played no part and over which the church had no control. Their vital interests were secularized as thoroughly as were the intellectual and cultural interests of the intelligentsia.

Catholic and Protestant religious life.—Even during these troubled centuries the energies of Christian people were not all expended in partisan and nationalistic struggles. There was piety, charity, and concern for the salvation of souls. Along with religious wars and controversies there were efforts to recover peace and unity among the churches.

A few of the men who worked for the reunion of the churches may be mentioned. Hugo Grotius, a Dutch

Arminian who is better known as "the father of international law," wrote a book entitled *A Way to Ecclesiastical Peace*. John Dury, born in Scotland and educated in Holland, spent a long lifetime traveling on the Continent and in England to promote the union of the churches. Rupertus Meldenius coined the slogan: "In things essential, unity; in things nonessential, liberty; in all things, charity." John Bergius, a liberal German Calvinist, was a leading advocate of church unity. George Calixtus, a liberal Lutheran, tried to find a way of union between Lutherans and Calvinists and also between these and Catholics. Spinola, a Spanish Catholic priest who went to Vienna and became bishop of Neustadt, exchanged views on union with Molanus, a Lutheran theologian. Leibnitz, the German philosopher, sent to Bossuet, a French Catholic bishop, the manuscript of a work by Molanus called *Private Thoughts concerning a Method of Reunion of the Protestant Church with the Roman Catholic Church*, and a long correspondence between Leibnitz and Bossuet ensued. The times were not propitious for the success of any of these efforts.

Catholic devotional and practical movements included the work of St. Francis de Sales, bishop of Geneva, who founded the Order of the Visitation to minister to the poor and sick and wrote an *Introduction to a Devout Life*, which ranks little below the *Imitation of Christ*, commonly attributed to Thomas à Kempis; Vincent de Paul, who organized the Sisters of Charity and, after working among the prisoners in the galleys, carried on mission work which led to the Congregation of Priests of the Mission; "Quietism," a mystical movement in which the great names were those of Molinos, Mme Guyon, and Fénelon; and the rise of the cult of the Sacred Heart of Jesus. Jansenism, originally a revival of Augustinian theology, came into sharp conflict with the teachings of the Jesuits and developed practices which brought it into official disfavor with the Catholic authorities. Pascal and Port Royal are memorable names in that connection.

Protestant Pietism in Germany developed from the work of Spener and Francke, who had come to believe that Lutheranism was emphasizing doctrine to the neglect of life. They cultivated a devotional mysticism with an emphasis upon personal religious "experience." The practical results were the building of charitable institutions, a new type of education both for the ministry and for the people, and the beginning of modern Protestant foreign missions. The Quaker movement in England, started by George Fox and promoted by William Penn, has much in common with Pietism, especially in the fervor of its devotional life; but, unlike Pietism, it cultivated an extreme separatism. Its members, seeking to avoid every form of worldliness, became a "peculiar people" in both senses; but their scrupulous honesty and their conscientious practice of nonresistance even in self-defense gradually won the respect of the community.

English Puritanism produced an intense devotion to a conception of religion including the principles of righteous government, a rigid code of private morality, and the practice of an austere but warm piety. Puritan preaching went far toward transforming the mind of England. Religious life was expressed and enriched by such widely different pieces of Puritan literature as Bunyan's *Pilgrim's Progress*, Milton's *Paradise Lost*, and Richard Baxter's *Saints' Everlasting Rest*.

Most important of all the devotional and practical movements within Protestantism was that initiated by John Wesley. An Anglican clergyman and an Oxford don, he came to feel that neither the established church nor any of the dissenting bodies offered the warm and heartfelt religion that he needed for his own soul and that the people of England needed to lift them out of formalism and indifference and to save them from wretchedness and immorality. His own crucial experience came when, at a meeting in Aldersgate Street, London, in 1738, he "felt his heart strangely warmed." It was no passing mood. For forty years thereafter he warmed the heart of England. Not until shortly before his death (1791) did Methodism definitely separate from the Church of England, though it had long developed independently of the mother-church to which Wesley continued to profess allegiance even while he defied its authority. Simultaneously there arose an evangelical movement in the Anglican church.

23. REVOLUTION AND REACTION

The French Revolution and religion.—The French Revolution began as a reasonable protest against a state of affairs in which all the social machinery was operated for the advantage of the privileged classes. It was not at first antireligious. The States-General, which met on May 4, 1789, opened with a mass and a sermon by a bishop, who spoke of the miseries of the poor and urged a reduction in taxation—but not too much reduction. Each of the three "estates" presented petitions, or complaints. The clergy consented to giving up exemption from taxation but insisted on retaining all their property and privileges, demanded the withdrawal of religious liberty and civil rights from Protestants, and the suppression of "infidel" books, condemned the suppression of any monastic houses, and asked control of all schools and colleges. The nobles were not averse to the privileges of the clergy (except exemption from taxation), favored the use of some monastic endowments for other purposes, and generally urged toleration of non-Catholics. The third estate (the commons) demanded complete religious freedom, expressed respect for the parish priests but criticized the higher clergy as "rich, idle, and avaricious," urged suppression of the smaller monasteries or of all not engaged in teaching or charity, asked the reduction or abolition of tithes, and demanded the cessation of all payments to Rome. In general, the commons wanted a free representative government, with civil and religious rights for all, in a Catholic monarchy.

The Declaration of the Rights of Man, adopted October 2, 1789, as the preamble of a constitution to be written later, declared for freedom of opinion and of worship and for the support of Catholic ministers and worship by the state. The revolution rapidly became more radical. The Republic established, the king and queen were executed, the church was completely subordinated to the state by a measure called "the civil constitution and the clergy," churches were closed or looted or secularized, a deistic "worship of the Supreme Being" was instituted (but little practiced), and for a short time the revolutionary government was in the hands of a little group of atheists who aimed at the complete eradication of religion.

Violent and bloody as the French Revolution was, atheism was not one of its characteristic features. It became and continued to be anticlerical. Its leaders revived a strain of skepticism which had for centuries been one element in the French tradition, rationalized it by accepting the teachings of the eighteenth-century philosophers (especially the Encyclopedists), and emotionalized it by associating it with the cause of humanity ("Liberty, Equality, and Fraternity") as against the church's championship of privilege, intolerance, and tyranny. Even the most ruthless directors of the Reign of Terror claimed to be acting in the interests of humanity. The revolutionary republic developed a kind of totalitarianism not unlike that of some modern states. Having overthrown a royal absolutism, it set up a more extreme absolutism of the state; and it did this in the name of liberty and the common good because it professed that the state represented the will and welfare of all the people. It held that "all independent corporations are evils to society," and since the church was the greatest of all independent corporations it must be reduced to the status of a mere branch of the public service occupied in teaching morals and dispensing charity. Since the church resisted this attack upon its autonomy—and even the lower clergy resisted, many of whom had been sympathetic with the humanitarian purposes of the revolution—church and state were aligned against each other as enemies. Later, when the revolution had been discredited and had been followed by reaction, the Catholic church was able to represent itself as having been the victim of a vicious assault by the foes of God and religion and as being the rallying point for a conservative and antidemocratic order in which alone lay safety.

Conservative reaction.—When revolutionary violence had spent its force, the pendulum swung back through successive phases of increasingly "strong" government—the Directory, the Napoleonic Consulate, the Napoleonic Empire. Napoleon's policy was to create a secular state embodying social equality, religious toleration, security for private property and civil rights, even-handed administration of justice, and non-interference by the church. His code of laws came nearer to realizing that ideal than anything that had existed in Europe since the fall of Rome and the rise of the papacy. He appreciated the values of religion as an instrument of social control, tried to subordinate the papacy to his purposes, entered into a concordat with the pope and brought him to Paris after he had destroyed the Papal State.

Napoleon's ruthless imperialism roused a coalition of all the European powers against him. His defeat was the signal for a general conservative reaction throughout Europe. An alliance of the "legitimate" princes (as distinguished from the upstart commoner who had made himself an emperor) undertook to throttle all liberal movements. Alexander I of Russia organized a "holy alliance" by the terms of which all rulers were to consider each other as brothers in Christ, their domains as parts of one great empire under the law of Christ, and their subjects as beloved children. So far as it had any effect (which was not much) it was to lend a sanction of piety to the measures that might be taken to check the rising tide of democracy. Yet the tide rose. There were widespread revolutions, with varying degrees of success in 1830 and 1849. For the most part these revolutions were put down. But if the frontal attacks upon governments generally failed, the spirit of democracy grew among the people, and many administrative reforms were gained.

When Napoleon's empire fell to pieces, the pope returned to Rome and to his sovereignty over the Papal State. The Jesuit order, which had been dissolved by Clement XIV in 1773 but which had maintained a secret existence, was restored and became a potent factor in the Catholic revival. It never again incurred such general odium as had led most of the Catholic powers to expel it before its dissolution. Until the papacy lost its temporal sovereignty in 1870, when Rome became the capital of the united kingdom of Italy, it continued to be the rallying point for organized opposition to all forms of political or intellectual liberalism and to denounce religious toleration as having no ground except indifference to religion.

Nevertheless, the Catholic church had a very genuine revival. High points in it were the Oxford movement in England (1845) which took Newman and many other Anglicans into the Church of Rome; the promulgation of the dogma of the Immaculate Conception of the Virgin Mary; the growth of the most popular shrine in Europe at Lourdes; the canonization of an unprecedented number of saints; the Vatican council (1870); and the dogma of papal infallibility.

European Protestantism.—European Protestantism in the nineteenth century had emerged from the stage in which its chief concerns were either to escape persecution or to inflict it upon other bodies of Protestants. French Protestants were at last completely free. The Scandinavian countries were so solidly and peacefully Lutheran that their religious history was uneventful. In Prussia, Lutherans and Reformed (Calvinists) were united (1817) to form the Evangelical church. The union had been promoted by pressure from the government, and not all of either party entered it. Germany had won the intellectual leadership of Europe—in philosophy, in science, and in historical and biblical scholarship. Protestant thought was open to all these influences. Being neither protected nor impeded by a censorship or an index of prohibited books, theologians could reconsider their views in the light of modern knowledge. A similar condition had already existed in England for a century. Of special importance were the effects produced upon religious thinking by the Kantian and post-Kantian philosophy, by discoveries in geology which proved that the earth was much older than the Book of Genesis seemed to indicate, by the theory of evolution, and by a new understanding of the nature of the Bible. On all these matters there arose various schools of thought the boundaries of which cut across the traditional denominational lines.

The civil disabilities which Catholics and nonconforming Protestants in England had borne through the eighteenth century were gradually removed. The old political battles between the papacy and the British government were sufficiently forgotten to permit the passage of the Catholic Emancipation Act (1829). Two ancient fictions were thus exploded: first, that the nation actually was united in the national church except for negligible minorities that could easily be excluded from political and civil rights; second, that it would be dangerous to admit these minorities (now seen to be considerable) to full participation in the national life.

24. SINCE 1870

Papal sovereignty.—The year 1870 was marked by great events which deeply affected the course of religion in Europe. That year saw the Franco-Prussian War, which led directly to the fall of the French Second Empire headed by Napoleon III; the rise of the Third Republic; and the organization of the German Empire under William I, who had been king of Prussia. The Holy Roman Empire, long dead, had been officially buried in 1806. The Second French Empire of Napoleon III, originating in an antirepublican revolution in 1852, had been strongly Catholic. In the republic which succeeded it the connection between

church and state was so slight that the disestablish-
ment of the church in 1905 produced scarcely a ripple.

The outbreak of the war between France and Prussia had necessitated the withdrawal of the French
troops from Rome, which was ready on that signal to
fall into the hands of Victor Emmanuel II, thus com-
pleting the unification of Italy and making the ancient
city the capital of the new kingdom. The Papal State,
which had already shrunk until its boundaries were the
city walls, was extinguished and the pope ceased to be
a temporal sovereign. Confining himself to the Vatican, the pope declared himself a prisoner and excommunicated the king. A state of tension continued to
exist between the papacy and the Italian government,
and the "Roman question" appeared to be an absolute deadlock. The popes refused to accept the settlement offered in the "Law of Guaranties" and insisted that they could not discharge their spiritual
functions without the status of sovereignty. Obviously
the Roman Catholic church could not have its headquarters elsewhere than at Rome, and just as obviously
Rome must be the capital of the kingdom of Italy.
Meanwhile the state, having had its origin in a liberal
democratic movement and in a drive to free the country from Austrian domination in the north, from the
rule of the Spanish Bourbons in the south, and from
clerical autocracy in the middle, developed along secular and liberal lines. Since it was difficult for the
people to be both patriotic and religious under such
conditions, most of them chose to be patriotic. Italy
remained nominally a Catholic country but with only

a minority of practicing Catholics. The deadlock on the Roman question was broken by the Lateran Treaty and the concordat of 1929, which set up a sovereign state of 105 acres, including little more than St. Peter's Cathedral, the Vatican, and its gardens. Mussolini, like Napoleon, recognized the value of religion as a social cement; unlike Napoleon, he was able to make a compromise which left the church its autonomy while gaining its blessing for the fascist state.

Bismarck, who had been the architect of the new German Empire, also undertook to reduce the Catholic church to the status of a government bureau. The May laws, by which the state undertook to decide who should be priests and bishops and how they should be trained, provoked a determined resistance which was called the Kulturkampf. It lasted until the death of Pius IX and the accession of Leo XIII, a man of more conciliatory temper, who made terms by which the church surrendered nothing of importance and the state receded from its unwise attempt to control the internal affairs of the church. The most important result of the Kulturkampf was that the "persecution" of the church quickened the zeal of many luke-warm Catholics, gave occasion for the founding of scores of Catholic newspapers (the "persecution" did not prevent that), and brought organized Catholicism into politics as a powerful "Center" party.

The churches and the social order.—The Protestant churches in Germany avoided the possibility of any clash with the secular power by confining their attention to doctrines and sacraments, the inculcation of private morality, and the maintenance of charitable institutions. They enjoyed the security and accepted the limitations implicit in their position under the patronage of the state, abstained from any interference with politics, and considered the social questions which had grown constantly more acute during the century as lying outside the church's proper field of interest. This policy, perhaps more consistently applied in Germany and the strongly Lutheran Scandinavian countries than elsewhere, was not confined to them.

In England, also, the established church took no leading part in promotion of social justice, in the granting of civil rights to non-Anglicans, in the correction of those political immoralities which were partly remedied by the Reform Bill (1832), in improving factory conditions and shortening the hours of child labor (to ten hours in 1847), or in removing the inhumanities of the colonial system. The dissenting churches did little more in the social field, though the proverbially sensitive "nonconformist conscience" was a factor in preparing the nation for these reforms.

The Christian Socialist movement is evidence that the churches were not wholly oblivious to the problems of labor and industry. In England it is chiefly associated with the names of J. F. D. Maurice and Charles Kingsley, both Anglican clergymen, who attempted to give a Christian motive and direction to the impulse which had to become explosive with the "Chartist" socialists. It was at least one of the roots from which later grew the interest of English Christians in social questions. Christian Socialism in Germany, rising later than the English movement but quite independent of it, got its positive program (or at least its stimulus to make a program) from Lassalle, a Jew who laid the foundations of the Social Democrat party, and found a large following among Catholics. Strangely enough, Christian Socialism in both Germany and Austria always had a bias toward anti-Semitism. The Catholic hierarchy in Germany were deeply interested in the movement and at one time believed that it might have the support of Rome. The sympathetic interest of Leo XIII in the condition of the working classes, as expressed in his encyclical *Rerum novarum* (1891), gave ground for this hope and helped to spread the movement in Italy, France, and Belgium. But the increasing aggressiveness of Marxian socialism, and the fear that preoccupation with social reforms would divert the attention of the faithful from the more important duties of campaigning for the restoration of papal sovereignty and avoiding the contamination of "modernism," caused both Leo XIII and his successor, Pius X, to withhold their favor, and Christian Socialism languished.

But the churches had done much toward creating the public opinion which supported the movements for social reform even though, as churches, they had taken no prominent part in them. Members of the churches were also citizens, and it is impossible to estimate how much of their humanitarian interest as citizens had its origin in attitudes they had learned as Christians.

By the beginning of the twentieth century the churches in Europe, as in America, were pervaded by a sentiment against war. They were beginning to make explicit pronouncements to the effect that war is contrary to the mind of Christ. The pacifist attitude that had been consistently maintained by the Quakers was not adopted by any other important group, but it was viewed sympathetically by many. Peace organizations drew a great part of their support from church members and had, in large part, a religious motivation. This peace sentiment grew strong in time of peace, but it could not stand the strain imposed upon it by the war of 1914–18. The established churches, having commitments to their states, naturally fell into line with the belligerent governments and found religious sanctions for their respective and opposing causes. Only in England were there strong dissenting churches, but these almost as promptly gave their approval. Still opposed to war in general as a savage and un-Christian way of adjusting international differences, they patriotically supported the state in *this* war as a righteous struggle against the forces of evil. Some of them thought of it as a "war to end war."

Between two wars.—The spiritual awakening which many had predicted as an outcome of the war did not come. Instead, there was a period of moral confusion. The churches, after all their patriotic service, were found to have lost prestige rather than to have gained. But even within those first post-war years, the British churches began to feel a new sense of responsibility for finding a Christian solution to the social and economic problems that came in the wake of the war. Never before had these questions been so diligently studied from

the standpoint of religion. During the twenty years between the two wars, few church conferences met without giving attention to these problems, and few ad-
journed without either adopting resolutions or ap-
pointing a committee to explore the possibilities of
remedying existing evils and creating a more Christian
social order.

The quickened awareness of the social implications
of religion was doubtless one influence which stimulated interest in co-operation and unity among the
churches. If Christianity had a social mission, it was
clearly one for which a divided church was inadequate.
Furthermore, the differences of doctrine and polity,
which furnished the historical ground for sectarian
divisions, seemed to be irrelevant to the social task.
Already it had been discovered that the world-wide
mission of the church demanded a closer union of its
forces. The impulse in this direction found notable expression in the World Conference on Missions held in
Edinburgh, Scotland, in 1910. Subsequent international and interdenominational assemblies in which
the ecumenical ideal was developed were the conferences on Life and Work at Stockholm (1925) and Oxford (1937) and on Faith and Order at Lausanne
(1927) and Edinburgh (1937) and the missions conferences at Jerusalem and Madras. These conferences
have included representatives of almost all churches
except the Roman Catholic. The wide discussion of
the reports of these conferences, the wealth of literature
which they have evoked, and the laying of foundations
for the World Council of Churches, all testify to the in-

terest in a closer fellowship of Christians and a more efficient organization for co-operation pending the time when a union of churches may be possible.

The rise of totalitarian states in recent years has presented to the churches new problems, the ultimate solution of which does not yet appear. Communist Russia has attempted to destroy the church and create a completely nonreligious society. Fascist Italy has sought to live on friendly terms with the dominant church, purchasing its favor by concessions and using it as a unifying element in the national life. Nazi Germany, making nationalism and racialism its real religion, has tried to reduce the churches, both Protestant and Catholic, to the status of obedient servants of the government, confining their activities to doctrine and the sacraments except as they emerge from their sanctuaries to render homage to the *Führer* and to support his policies. The immediate outcome of this plan hinges upon the turn of fortune in the present European war. Its ultimate issues can be foreseen in the light of the successive failures, though sometimes long deferred, of all previous efforts to subordinate the church to the purposes of politics and war.

CHAPTER VII

CHRISTIANITY IN THE AMERICAS

25. How Christianity Came to America

Religion played an essential part in the settlement and development of the American colonies. It is historically significant that the discovery of America and the beginning of the Protestant Reformation came within twenty-five years of each other and that eventually practically every religious body in western Europe which arose out of the Reformation sent representatives to the New World. In fact, it is not far wrong to say that Colonial America was the chief refuge for Europeans persecuted for conscience. But Colonial America was more than a religious refuge, for politics, economics, and social motives had their part in bringing colonists, and religion so often tied in with these other motives that it is difficult to separate one from another.

The Church of England in the colonies.—One of the principal religious bodies to be transplanted to America during the Colonial period was the Church of England. Being the church established by law in the mother-country, it was the policy of the English officials to give it all possible assistance in the colonies. Several of the colonies were established by men who were very loyal churchmen, and, of course, they were anxious that their church should have all the advantages in the New

World that they could possibly secure for it. So it happened that in every one of the colonies which had not been established by dissenters the Church of England succeeded in gaining legal establishment. Virginia was the the oldest of these Church of England colonies, but later Maryland, North and South Carolina, New York, and Georgia all passed laws providing that the Church of England should be the official church. This meant very little, however, outside Virginia, for from the beginning in the other colonies dissenting groups were more numerous.

Of great importance to the Church of England in the colonies was the founding in 1701 of the great missionary society called the Society for the Propagation of the Gospel in Foreign Parts, often called the S.P.G. The purpose of this organization, which is still in existence, was to send missionaries to English colonists wherever they were to be found. During the period from 1702 to the close of the Revolution this society sent three hundred and ten missionaries to the American colonies, and they labored in every colony save Virginia. Virginia needed no missionaries, since the church was so well established there that it could get on without help. Many of these missionaries performed a noble service and lived sacrificial lives, but some of the ministers, especially those in Virginia and Maryland, neglected their parish duties, often doing more harm than good.

In New England the Church of England got a rather slow start, since the Congregationalists were hostile to it and did all they could to keep it out. It was not until Massachusetts became a royal colony in 1689 that the first Episcopalian church was founded in Boston. After that, through the assistance of the S.P.G., it secured a foothold in the other New England colonies. A happening that gave great impetus to the church in Connecticut was the conversion in 1722 to the Episcopal church of Timothy Cutler, the president of Yale College, and of Samuel Johnson with several other Connecticut Congregational ministers. Cutler became the minister of the second Episcopal church in Boston and Samuel Johnson became the first president of King's College. In the colonies where Quaker influence was dominant the Church of England soon gained a foothold, and Philadelphia became a strong center of Church of England influence. At the end of the Colonial period the Church of England ranked fourth among the religious bodies in America, with four hundred and eighty congregations. It had two colleges, William and Mary in Virginia, founded in 1692, and King's College in New York, the former being the second oldest college in North America. The English church was greatly handicapped throughout the Colonial period because it was not successful in securing a bishop for America. The bishop of London attempted to exercise some episcopal supervision, but he was too far away to perform that function adequately.

Colonial Congregationalism.—In the three New England colonies—Massachusetts, Connecticut, and New Hampshire—the Congregational church was established by law, and the ministers were paid by levies made upon the people as a whole. The first Congregational church was established at Plymouth, Massachusetts, by the little group of Separatist Puritans who came from Holland in the "Mayflower" in 1620. A great Puritan immigration began in 1628 which lasted until 1640, and, as new towns sprang up around Boston harbor, new congregations were formed. The leaders among these new settlers had been members of the Church of England in the mother-country, but, on coming to America, they adopted the Congregational form of church government. In about ten years thirty-three Congregational churches were formed. The Congregational ministers exercised a powerful political influence, though they held no political office. The first Congregational book of discipline, called the Cambridge Platform, was adopted in 1648. It embodied the doctrinal parts of the Calvinistic Westminster Confession of Faith.

During the Colonial period the Congregationalists founded three colleges with the primary purpose of training a ministry for their churches: Harvard, established in 1636; Yale, in 1701; and Dartmouth, in 1770. Of great importance to Congregationalism was the adoption in 1662 of the Halfway Covenant providing for a kind of halfway church membership for those who did not profess a religious experience, which was true of a majority of the third generation. These halfway church members tended to increase, which gave rise to a growing religious inertia and helps account for liberal tendencies which began to manifest themselves toward the close of the seventeenth century. To check these tendencies, the Massachusetts leaders proposed the creation of organizations resembling presbyteries. These were rejected in Massachusetts but were adopted in Connecticut and were embodied in what is known as the Saybrook Platform of 1708. From this time forward Connecticut Congregationalism tended to become more and more Presbyterian, a fact which later had far-reaching effects in causing Connecticut Congregationalists and Presbyterians to unite in numerous enterprises.

The Colonial Presbyterians.—Ranking in importance and numbers with the two established churches, were the Presbyterians and the Baptists. Previous to the great Scotch-Irish immigration to the colonies, which began about the beginning of the eighteenth century, there were few Presbyterian congregations in the colonies. Some of the Puritans who had come to New England favored the Presbyterian form of church government, and a number of these had migrated to Long Island, where several Presbyterian congregations were established. But the rapid increase of Presbyterianism in America began with the coming of the Scotch-Irish.

These Presbyterian Irish were of Scotch blood, having come to northern Ireland as colonists as a result of the policy instituted by England of controlling the turbulent Irish Catholics. They made excellent colonists, and soon their part of Ireland was the most prosperous section of that island. But toward the end of the seventeenth century the English government began to place economic restrictions upon them, and that together with the rise in rents and the necessity of paying tithes to support the Episcopal church in Ireland caused great discontent, and by 1720 they were coming to America in great waves. By 1750 it has been estimated that a hundred thousand had come to America, and they were found in every one of the thirteen colonies in sufficient numbers to make their influence felt. Having come late to the colonies, they made their homes most frequently in the back country and constituted America's first frontiersmen. They were practically 100 per cent Presbyterian, so that their coming soon raised Presbyterianism to prominence.

Francis Makemie, a Scotch-Irish missionary, is called the father of American Presbyterianism, because it was largely through his efforts that the first presbytery in America was formed in 1706. This was the Philadelphia presbytery. In 1716 the first synod was organized consisting of four presbyteries, and by 1730 there were thirty Presbyterian ministers in America. In order to meet the growing demand for ministers, the Presbyterians established in 1746 the College of New Jersey, now Princeton University. This had been preceded by a school known as the "Log College" which had been carried on at Neshaminy, Pennsylvania, by an Irish Presbyterian minister, William Tennent. The College of New Jersey grew rapidly and by the end of the Colonial period had turned out more than a hundred and fifty zealous young ministers. Among the Colonial churches the Presbyterian ranked second only to the Congregationalists in number of congregations, having 543 with the opening of the War for Independence.

The Baptists in Colonial America.—In point of numbers the Baptists ranked among the four largest of the Colonial religious bodies. The English Baptists were an offshoot of the Puritan movement and are closely related in their origins to the beginnings of Congregationalism. In America Baptist ideas appeared first in Massachusetts, and Roger Williams is generally considered as the father of American Baptists. It is doubtful if Williams was ever immersed, though he held to the other great Baptist principles of separation of church and state, believer's baptism, conversion as a condition of membership, the complete independence of the congregation, and individual responsibility to God. The church he formed at Providence, Rhode Island, is considered by the Baptists as the mother-church. The Baptist church grew slowly in New England but got a firm foothold in the Middle Colonies through the immigration of Welsh and English Baptists. There were also some early congregations in Virginia and Maryland. But the great growth of the American Baptists did not come until the great Colonial revivals, which we will discuss in a separate place.

The smaller Colonial churches.—Besides these four largest Colonial religious bodies—the Church of England, the Congregationalists, the Presbyterians, and the Baptists—Quakers were pretty well scattered throughout all the colonies; the Dutch Reformed church was found where the Dutch settled along the Hudson and on Long Island and in and about New York City; the German Reformed, the Lutherans, and the several small German bodies—the Mennonites, the Dunkers, the Schwenkfelders, and the Moravians—were more numerous in Pennsylvania than anywhere else, since Pennsylvania had been most hospitable to the German settlers, though they were also found in New York, Maryland, and Georgia. There were also about 50 congregations of Roman Catholics, the largest number being found in Maryland, though Pennsylvania contained considerable numbers. Of the other smaller bodies, the Quakers had 295 congregations; the Dutch and German Reformed together, 251; the Lutherans, 151; the Moravians, 6 or 8, while the Mennonites and Dunkers had perhaps some 20 each.

Old World connections of the Colonial churches.—All these religious bodies found in the American colonies were transplantations from Europe, and several of them had Old World connections. Thus the Anglicans were under the supervisions of the bishop of London and the S.P.G.; the Presbyterians looked to the General Assembly of Scotland, at least for precedents, just as the Quakers looked to the Yearly Meeting of London; the Catholics were under the supervision of the Vicar Apostolic in London and the Congregation of Propaganda in Rome; the Dutch and German Reformed bodies were more or less under the direction of the Classis or Presbytery of Amsterdam; while the Lutherans looked to the University of Halle for advice and assistance, and the Moravians were under the direction of the Moravian authorities at Herrnhut. The Congregationalists, the Baptists, the Mennonites, and Dunkers were self-contained and had no connection with directing bodies in the Old World.

Colonial revivals and their influence.—From the standpoint of all the colonies and of religion in general the great Colonial revivals rank as the most important religious movement of the whole Colonial period. Up to that time religion had been very largely the concern of the few, while the great mass of the people were out of touch with the church. Beginning in 1734 in New England, under the preaching of Jonathan Edwards at Northampton, Massachusetts, the revival swept pretty generally throughout the colonies. In New England the revival added at least twenty-five thousand new church members. In the middle colonies, under the preaching of Presbyterian revivalists particularly, it stirred the religious life as never before. In the southern colonies the revival began about 1750 and continued in three successive waves to the Revolution. In its first phase it was largely a Presbyterian movement and marked the beginning of Presbyterianism in the South. In its second phase it was largely a Baptist movement, resulting in the rapid rise of the Baptist denomination to a place of importance in Virginia and North Carolina particularly. In its third phase it marked the beginning of Methodism in America. George Whitefield, who made six evangelistic tours of the colonies from 1740 to 1770, ranged up and down the colonies and in a sense tied the Colonial revivals into one great movement. Many influences came out of the revivals, besides that of increasing church membership. They led directly and indirectly to the founding of several colleges. The College of New Jersey, the College of Rhode Island, Dartmouth, the College of Philadelphia, Queen's College, and King's College all arose during the revival years. The revivals were also the first great intercolonial movement and had much to do in drawing the thirteen colonies together. They also gave rise to a new leadership among the common people, as the Baptist and Methodist revivals were largely lay movements.

The churches and the War for Independence.—The Colonial churches played an important role in winning independence. The Congregationalists, the Presbyterians, and the Baptists were almost a unit in their support of the patriot cause. It has been pointed out in recent studies that the Congregational ministers of New England were preaching the philosophy of the American Revolution for a hundred years previous to the Revolution. When war came, Congregationalists were naturally found on the patriot side. The Scotch-Irish Presbyterians were equally unanimous in their support, since they but recently had come to America to escape the restrictions which England had placed upon them in northern Ireland. The Baptists, advocates of liberty par excellence, seized the occasion of the war to urge not only independence from England but also a larger degree of religious freedom in America. The German and the Dutch churches were also largely American in their sympathies. Several of the sons of Henry M. Mühlenberg, the father of American Lutheranism, became particularly conspicuous as leaders in the cause. The pacifist sects such as the Quakers, the Moravians, the Dunkers, and the Mennonites were loyal to America but refused to take a part in the fighting and thereby suffered severe persecution. The Catholics were also generally patriots. Of all the American churches the Episcopalian suffered most. The royal governors and other Colonial officials were usually Church of England men, and the church contained numerous Loyalists. On the other hand, there were more Episcopalians who signed the Declaration of Independence than of any other Colonial church. John Witherspoon, the Presbyterian president of the College of New Jersey, was the only minister to sign the Declaration.

26. How the Churches Developed from the War of Independence to the Civil War

Severing the Old World connections.—The first great task which faced the American churches after the achievement of independence was that of severing Old World connections, establishing themselves as distinctly American bodies, and writing into the fundamental law of the land the great principle of the separation of church and state. Congregationalism was little affected by the new nationalizing tendencies, and, instead of a movement toward centralization, a movement in the opposite direction was abroad. Baptists, though congregational in polity, nevertheless developed a distinct national consciousness, even though they lacked a national organization. Previous to the Revolution Methodism in America, as in England, was a movement within the Episcopal church carried on by lay preachers. Because the failure of the Episcopal clergy in America to co-operate, John Wesley took steps to form them into a separate church, and in 1784, the Methodist Episcopal church was organized.

The Presbyterians began the formation of a national organization in 1785, and by 1788 this had been accomplished with the formation of the Presbyterian church in the United States of America. The Episcopal church, under the leadership of Rev. Dr. William White of Philadelphia, the rector of Christ Church, was the principal leader in forming a national body, and by 1788 the Protestant Episcopal church had been organized with three American bishops consecrated in England and Scotland. The Roman Catholic church secured their first American bishop, John Carroll, in 1790. The Lutherans began to gather their churches into separate state organizations in 1786; the Dutch Reformed church completed its national organization in 1792, and the German Reformed church the following year, 1793.

Following populations westward.—The most immediate concern of the American churches after their formation into national bodies was that of following the population as it pushed westward from the Atlantic seaboard into the center of the continent. This movement of population began immediately on the close of the Revolution and continued until the entire continent had been peopled. By 1821 eleven new states had been admitted to the Union, and by 1860 states were rapidly coming into being west of the Mississippi; California had been admitted to statehood, and territories were organizing in the far Northwest.

Presbyterians and the frontier.—Those churches which met these problems most successfully were those which naturally became the largest Protestant religious bodies in America. The Presbyterians, the Baptists, and the Methodists were the most successful in dealing with frontiers. The Presbyterians, with their long tradition of an educated ministry and their rigid creed and form of church government, were handicapped to a certain degree by their high standards and rigid confession. Thus they were not able to supply an educated ministry for all the many new communities arising in the West, while their insistence upon strict obedience to their creed and polity caused dissension and finally division. The Cumberland Presbyterian church was a frontier division (1810). The Presbyterians contributed large numbers to the movement which became the Church of the Disciples, through such leaders as Thomas and Alexander Campbell and Barton W. Stone, all of whom were Presbyterians. Though failing to gain as large a membership as did the Baptists and Methodists, the Presbyterians made the largest contribution to education in the early West, since the Presbyterian ministers constituted the largest single body of college graduates on the early frontier, and the first schools and colleges were naturally formed by them.

Baptist and Methodist frontier methods.—Because of their uneducated and unsalaried ministry and their democratic form of church government, the Baptists made a very large appeal to frontier people, especially those moving westward from the southern states. In

order to form a frontier Baptist church, it was not necessary to ask the consent of any official body, as each
Baptist church elected and ordained its own minister.
Nor were large sums of money necessary to erect a
church building, for the frontier spirit of co-operation
was all that was needed to bring that about, so that the
poverty of the pioneers was no handicap in the propagation of the Baptist gospel. So it came about that
wherever Baptist people settled there was sure to arise
before very long a Baptist church. Thus the Baptist
denomination was carried along with the settlers, and
it may be said that no other religious body seemed to
spring so naturally out of the soil of the frontier.

Equally effective with the Baptists as a frontier
church were the Methodists. Their circuit-rider system
devised by John Wesley in England was brought to
America by Asbury and proved to be ideally suited to
the carrying-on of religious work among a restless and
moving population. The circuit system made it possible for one preacher to cover a vast territory, the
early circuits often taking the rider six weeks to make
one round, preaching almost every day in the week at a
different place. The highly centralized Methodist system of supervision, by bishops and presiding elders,
and the method of sending men here and there wherever they were most needed, enabled Methodism to
keep pace with the moving frontier. The Methodist
gospel was also well suited to a democratic society,
since it emphasized free grace and individual responsibility to God. When in about 1830 the Disciples of
Christ became an independent denomination, they too

became a particularly successful frontier church and by 1860 had a membership of more than five hundred thousand.

Episcopalians and Congregationalists on the frontier.— The Episcopalians and the Congregationalists were late in adopting any adequate method of following population west and, as a result, lagged behind the other churches in winning large memberships. It was not until 1835 that the Episcopalians adopted a frontier missionary policy, and by that time the religious pattern of the West had been largely fixed. It was not until cities and large towns began to arise in the West that the Episcopal church began to grow nationally. The Congregationalists united with the Presbyterians in a Plan of Union in 1801, by which they agreed to co-operate on the frontier. But the net result of this plan was to increase Presbyterianism at the expense of Congregationalism, since Presbyterianism with its more highly centralized church government tended to absorb the more loosely governed Congregationalists.

Revivalism.—All the so-called "evangelical" churches were greatly influenced by revivalism throughout the nineteenth century, and the Baptist, the Congregational, the Presbyterian, the Disciple, and the Methodist bodies particularly used this method of winning people to the Christian life and church membership. The great western revival which began in Kentucky in 1797 and swept throughout the West, and indeed throughout the country, was an interdenominational movement of widespread influence. It fixed the pattern of revivalism for the next century. Even the Episcopalian, the Lutheran, and the Reformed churches used revivalistic methods to a limited degree. On the frontier the camp meeting became the most important social and religious institution. Begun by the Presbyterians in Kentucky in the early days of the great western revival, it was developed particularly by the Methodists and helps explain why Methodism forged ahead of other bodies in the West. Other churches continued to use the camp meeting, as did the Cumberland Presbyterians and Baptists.

The churches and the college movement.—As the churches grew throughout the country, and particularly in the West, the demand for ministers likewise grew, and the churches began to establish academies and colleges for the training of ministers as well as schools for general educational purposes. By 1860 the American churches had established 180 colleges in the United States. The Presbyterians had founded 49; the Methodists, 34; the Baptists, 25; the Congregationalists, 21; the Catholics, 14; the Episcopalians, 11; the Lutherans, 6; and the Disciples, 5; while seven other denominations had established 15 others. In 1860 there were but 27 colleges and universities in the United States that were not founded or controlled by religious bodies, and several of these, such as the early state institutions, were largely under the control of ministers. Thus the whole pattern of higher education in America to the Civil War was shaped by the religious bodies.

The era of organization.—The period from 1800 to 1830 may be called the era of organization and is characterized by religious activity on a wide scale. It was during these years that home and foreign missionary activity was getting under way, and the formation of missionary societies, both denominational and inter-denominational, followed one another in rapid succession. By 1820 all the major religious bodies had both active home and foreign missionary agencies. Such interdenominational organizations as the American Bible Society (1816), the American Sunday School Union (1824), the American Tract Society (1825), and others of like nature, arose to meet the problems created by the great western movement. From this period also dates the rise of theological seminaries, and by 1840 there were at least twenty-five seminaries engaged in training a ministry for the various Protestant bodies.

The era of controversy.—The period from 1830 to 1860 is filled with growing controversy and division among the churches in America. None of the major religious bodies was exempt. The Catholics were increasing rapidly as a result of growing immigration from Ireland and Germany, thereby arousing fears that American institutions were in danger. This led to an anti-Catholic movement and gave rise to an anti-Catholic political party known as the American or Know-Nothing party. At the same time the Catholics were having trouble over what is called "trusteeism," which arose when certain Catholic laymen attempted to control Catholic churches, following the example of their Protestant neighbors. Eventually the Catholic bishops triumphed and their churches remained in clerical hands. The public-school question also was a disturbing factor, the Catholics claiming the right to receive state aid for their parochial schools. Controversy in the Protestant Episcopal church arose between High Church and Low Church parties, and a pamphlet warfare was carried on for many years over this issue. The Presbyterians divided in 1837–38 over several issues growing out of the Plan of Union with the Congregationalists, forming independent Old School and New School bodies. The Lutherans were agitated over the language question and confessionalism, a tension which was rendered more acute by the coming of many new conservative Lutherans from Germany after 1830. The greatest cause of controversy and schism, however, was the slavery issue.

The institution of Negro slavery became increasingly important economically and politically after the invention of the cotton gin in 1792. Previous to this event the leaders in the nation, both North and South, were quite generally in favor of getting rid of the institution, but by 1830 a far-reaching agricultural revolution had taken place in the South, fastening slavery upon that region more tenaciously than ever before. At the same time a radical antislavery movement was under way in the North, and thus the two sections grew farther and farther apart in their views of the slavery question. Since the churches are made up of citizens, it was found impossible to keep the slave issue out of the churches. As a result all the Protestant churches that were more or less equally distributed in both North and South divided over the issue. The Presbyterians had divided first (1837), owing to the fact that other issues were involved. In 1857 the New School divided into northern and southern branches. In 1844 and 1845 the Methodists and Baptists divided, and, when the Civil War came, the Episcopalians, the Lutherans, and the Old School Presbyterians formed churches in the Confederate States. The Congregationalists, since they were almost entirely a northern body, did not divide; nor did the Disciples. There was little slavery controversy among the Catholics and no division, since their central authority was located outside the United States.

The opening of the Civil War marked the end of an era in the history of the American churches, just as it did in the political and economic life of the nation.

27. Religion in the United States since the Civil War

The churches on both sides of the great civil struggle of 1861–65 supported devotedly their respective sections. In fact, the support of the churches actually increased sectional bitterness, for when religious bodies go to war they often forget or at least lay aside the principles of the Prince of Peace. After the war the great mass of church members in the North supported the mistaken reconstruction policies which fastened military and carpet bag rule on the South for nearly ten years following the cessation of hostilities. This was one of the reasons why the unification of churches severed by slavery and the war has been so slow.

The freedmen and the rise of Negro churches.—The problems of the reconstruction years were many and difficult. One was that of dealing with the freedmen. During the war freedmen's aid societies had sprung up all over the North, and when the war came to a close church agencies were soon occupied in sending missionaries and teachers into the South to bring religion and education to the great mass of ignorant Negroes just released from slavery. This work has been continued and is one of the most significant factors in the economic, social, and cultural progress of the Negro race. The rapid rise of independent Negro churches was also going on during reconstruction years. Baptist and Methodist churches made the largest appeal to the Negro, with the result that the African Methodist, the African Methodist Zion, the Colored Methodist Episcopal, and the Negro Baptists soon had churches throughout the South. In 1930 the Negro Baptists numbered about 3,750,000, and the combined membership of the three independent Negro Methodist churches was about 1,500,000.

Immigration and the settlement of the prairie states.—Another post–Civil War church activity was that of helping to plant churches in the new states and territories in the prairie and Rocky Mountain regions. Movement of population into trans-Missouri gave rise to a new kind of church organization, the church extension societies; these societies, however, did not duplicate the many home missionary agencies. They were made necessary by the scarcity and high cost of building materials in regions devoid of timber. These regions also contained the largest proportion of the Indian population in the nation; and, as settlers pushed into the

Indian country, Indian restlessness resulted leading to serious Indian outbreaks in the Dakotas, Minnesota, Montana, and Wyoming. These disturbances brought Indians to the renewed attention of the churches and led in turn to an increased missionary activity among them. In 1923 there were about six hundred and fifty missionaries of all religious complexions engaged in missionary work among the Indians in the United States.

Beginning in the seventies a vast new immigration, to a large extent Scandinavian, was pushing into the central Northwest. This led to the formation of independent Scandinavian Lutheran churches, such as the Norwegian synod, the Augustana synod (Swedish), and the United Danish synod. The German immigration previous to the Civil War resulted in the formation of several large German Lutheran bodies, the Missouri, Wisconsin, Ohio, and Iowa synods being the most important. Of the religious bodies in the United States the Lutherans, the Catholics, and the Jews profited most from nineteenth- and twentieth-century immigration. The Scandinavian Lutherans alone now number about a million members, while the recent German Lutherans have at least one and a half million members. Immigration from eastern and southern Europe since 1880 has been responsible for many millions of Catholics. About five millions of the Catholic increase in the United States since 1880 has been due to immigration alone. It was this vast influx of Catholics which gave rise to the anti-Catholic movement in the eighties known as the American Protective Association, which ran the usual course of such movements. Jewish congregations in the United States showed a rapid increase in the last half-century. In 1890 there were 533 Jewish congregations in the United States; in 1926 there were 3,118; and in recent years the number has increased rapidly.

Evolution and higher criticism.—Protestant Christianity particularly was compelled to adjust itself in the years following the Civil War to new views of creation, known as the evolutionary theory, as set forth by Charles Darwin in the *Origin of Species* and the *Descent of Man*, and to new views of the Bible as brought out in the work of a group of biblical scholars, known as the higher critics. Higher criticism is the testing of the authenticity of the Bible by the same methods that scholars use in the testing of any other body of ancient literature. Both were disturbing factors and both continued to be so for a generation, or until well past the turn of the twentieth century. Immediately after the war of 1914–18 these same issues were revived in the fundamentalist-modernist controversy. This divided the evangelical churches into two opposing camps, thus threatening for a while a serious schism in all the larger churches. These controversies, however, only slightly affected the Catholics and the Lutherans, both bodies clinging tenaciously to their ancient positions.

Growing wealth and the rise of the social gospel.—Perhaps the most far-reaching changes in recent years in organized Christianity in America have been brought about directly or indirectly as a result of the vastly increased wealth of the nation as a whole. As the wealth of the nation grew, the wealth and general culture of the churches likewise increased. Methodists and Baptists particularly, which had made their greatest early contributions as the churches of the poor, were becoming rapidly the churches of the upper middle class. As a result, the old revivalistic methods which had been so successful in the earlier years were now being discarded, and a more formal worship began to displace the "free and easy" worship of the earlier time. These changes were particularly responsible for the rise of many new revivalistic sects often called the "Holy Rollers" which began to appear about 1880 and have continued to increase down to the present time. Still another effect of growing wealth was the increased alienation of the working classes from the churches. This situation was brought to the particular attention of the church since about 1890 through the rise of what has come to be termed the "social-gospel emphasis." The leaders in this movement have called attention to the necessity of making a practical application of the principles of Jesus to the industrial problems of our time. Some of the most able among religious leaders of the last generation have been men who have emphasized this phase of Christianity. All the larger churches have adopted social creeds, and several of them have established organizations to put their creeds into practice.

The war of 1914–18 and its aftermath.—Since the war of 1914–18 no subject has been more constantly before the people than world-peace. The churches have taken a leading part in this movement, and many ministers have definitely identified themselves as out-and-out pacifists. Recent developments in Europe and the rise of militant naziism have caused considerable modification of pacifist attitudes on the part of many Christian leaders, though the pacifist position has by no means been abandoned by the church, as at least an ideal for Christians.

The period following the war of 1914–18 was one of general disillusionment and affected every phase of American life, political, social, economic, moral, and religious. The idealism which had brought America into the war, which made possible national prohibition and stimulated the great money campaigns in the churches to save the world in a generation, was soon dispelled. Americans were through trying to save the world, especially since the world refused to be saved by their efforts, and they now turned their attention to their own needs and pleasures, with large emphasis upon pleasures. They repudiated the League of Nations, laid high tariffs on imports, and instituted an extreme isolationist policy in national affairs. The great missionary plans for the world were crippled when church people began to curtail their giving for missions, and soon the whole foreign missionary enterprise was under a growing cloud of criticism if not of suspicion. National prohibition was repealed, and the cocktail and the tipsy era was ushered in, sweeping along with it many church members, formerly advocates of the dry cause.

The decade of the twenties, which may be designated as the extravagant era, witnessed vast expenditures for churches, colleges, universities, hospitals, and other religious and charitable institutions. All this was going on while missionary giving was declining. As a consequence the churches overexpanded in just the same way that business overexpanded. And the same results followed, when the depression came, with the thirties. Many colleges closed their doors; others were forced to dismiss large numbers of their teaching staff; ministers' salaries declined or were left unpaid. On the other hand, there were some permanent gains. The rise of beautiful church buildings all over the nation was a permanent acquisition and has been one of the factors in the increasing emphasis upon dignifying worship.

Recent changes in the theological scene.—A rebirth of interest in theology was one of the consequences of the war of 1914–18. It was first noticeable in arousing a new interest in spiritualism and premillennialism, the former on the part of those hoping to be able to commune with dear ones lost in the great war, while the latter was the natural result of the terrible holocaust which was drenching the battlefields of Europe with blood and which seemed to many to presage the speedy end of all things. Millennialism not only found advocates among the small sects but permeated widely most of the larger Protestant bodies and was one of the prime factors in building up the fundamentalist movement. The years of prosperity brought with them a new humanism, growing out of an impatience with the too easy cures for the pains of the world advocated by many church leaders. The new humanists played down God and played up man, the more extreme wing denying the personality of God. But the depression years slowed down this movement, and soon theology was swinging in the opposite direction, setting forth a view of God as transcendent, who alone can transform the structure of human society, and leaving man with nothing more to do than to wait on God's good time to make a better world. This type of Christian thought has come largely out of Europe, particularly from the Swiss theologian Karl Barth, and has been promoted by an able group of young American theologians. This emphasis runs counter to American experience and background and has been stoutly resisted by liberal theologians generally.

Church union.—The fact that in the United States there are more than two hundred separate denominations has been a growing concern among an increasing number of Christian leaders of all the major churches. But the ideal of Christian union is an old one, in the United States as well as in the Christian church as a whole. A long step was taken in the direction of Protestant co-operation when in 1905 the Federal Council of the Churches of Christ in America was drawn up and three years later was ratified by thirty churches. In 1865 the Protestant Episcopal church was able to heal the schism created by the Civil War, and in 1868 the Old School and New School Presbyterians united in the North to form the Presbyterian church in the United States. In 1906 the Cumberland Presbyterians of the North also united with the larger Presbyterian body. The year 1911 marks the union of the Free Will

Baptists and the Northern Baptists. In 1917 the Norwegian Lutheran church of America was created by the merging of three formerly independent bodies, and in 1918 the great United Lutheran church was created by the union of the General Council, the General Synod, and the United Synod of the South, the latter having been a Civil War division. In 1920 the Presbyterian church was successful in drawing into its folds the Welsh Calvinistic Methodist church; two years later (1922) the division among the Evangelical bodies was healed when the Evangelical church was formed. The German Reformed church in 1924 united with the Hungarian Reformed church and in 1934 merged with the Evangelical synod to form the Evangelical and Reformed church. The Congregationalists likewise have been a party to two unifications in recent years, the first in 1924, when they united with a group of German Evangelical churches, composed of German people who had come out of Russia since 1870, the second, in 1931, when they united with the Christian churches, the latter being one of the bodies which had come out of the New Light movement on the frontier. Largest of all the unification movements in American Protestantism and perhaps the largest in the history of Protestantism was that consummated in 1939 with the forming of the Methodist church as a happy result of the merging of the Methodist Episcopal, the Methodist Episcopal Church South, and the Methodist Protestant church. This merger creates a church of nearly eight million members. Let us hope that unification movements will continue until the torn garment of Christ shall once more be whole.

Christian leaders in America were not interested merely in drawing together the numerous religious bodies in the United States; they also joined heartily in the movement to bring about world-wide unity. This has resulted in a series of world-conferences, the most notable being the Stockholm Conference of 1925, the Lausanne Conference of 1927, and ten years later the great gatherings of Christian leaders at Oxford and Edinburgh. In these great meetings Christians representing different communions have learned to talk together and to listen with interest and appreciation to other points of view. The World Council of Churches is now being formulated as the most recent expression of this ecumenical spirit.

28. CHRISTIANITY IN HISPANIC AMERICA AND IN CANADA

Colonization of South and Central America.—The colonization of South and Central America by the Spanish and Portuguese began more than a hundred years before England was ready to plant her first colonies on American soil. Thus the second voyage of Columbus was a great colonizing expedition made up of seventeen ships and resulted in the founding of the first permanent Spanish colony in the New World, on the north shore of the island of Santo Domingo, which the Spaniards called Hispaniola, or "Little Spain." The Spanish colonies spread rapidly through the larger islands of the West Indies, and in 1509 the colonization of the mainland was begun on the Isthmus of Panama. By 1525 Mexico had been conquered by Cortez, and ten years later the city of Lima was founded by Francisco Pizarro in the midst of his conquest of Peru. By the end of the century the Spaniards had planted their main centers on the west coast of South America, and the Portuguese had successfully begun their great Brazilian colony.

All this colonizing activity had been done in connection with Roman Catholicism, for the planting of the *Santa Fé* or "holy faith" was one of the main objects of the Catholic kings in all their colonizing enterprises. In fact, the early Spanish *conquistadores* considered themselves Christian crusaders and brought over to the New World the ideas which had grown up in the long wars which they had fought against the Moors in Spain, using the same battle cries and evoking the same saints in the New World that had served them in the old. Priests accompanied practically all conquering and colonizing expeditions, and the conversion of the natives went on in conjunction with their conquest and exploitation.

Catholic missionary activity.—It is most astonishing how quickly literally thousands of natives were brought to an outward acceptance of Christianity by the many Franciscan, Dominican, Capuchin, Augustinian, and Jesuit missionaries who flocked to the New World to bring it into subjection to the Kingdom of Christ. During the earlier conquests the church and the padres were largely the tools of the unscrupulous conquerors. These early expeditions were little more than filibustering expeditions of adventurers, who risked their own money and lives in the hope of profit. In these expeditions the priests helped to gain and keep the royal favor and were often of great assistance in securing the easy submission of the Indians. The later missionaries, however, came out usually entirely independent of the political authorities, and a higher and better type of work among the Indians was the result. Tribes of Indians were assigned to each order, and the friars went out to establish missions in remote regions far distant from the Spanish settlements. The Indians were gathered into missions called *Reductions*, where schools were opened and instruction given in the simpler arts and in Christian doctrine. Among the most famous of these missions were those established by the Jesuits in Paraguay, though Catholic missions were wide flung throughout the Spanish and Portuguese colonial empires. Padre Junipero Serra, with a band of Franciscans, began the Christian conquest of California in 1769, and by his death in 1784 he had founded nine separate mission establishments. Perhaps the greatest figure in Hispanic America in the colonial period was Bartolomé de Las Casas (1474–1566), "the Apostle to the Indians," a Dominican friar who devoted his life to the welfare of the natives and well deserves the title by which he is universally known.

Catholic organization and wealth in colonial America.— Besides the work carried on by the missionaries to the Indians the Catholic church was firmly established in every one of the Spanish and Portuguese American colonial centers. Each of the larger towns became the head of a bishopric while the larger cities became archiepiscopal centers. Thus by the end of the eighteenth century there were seven archbishops and forty-one bishops in Spanish and Portuguese America. In the course of the years Roman Catholicism came to control a good share of the wealth of the colonies. In 1810 there were in Spanish America 552 convents. In 1620 the viceroy of Peru told Philip III that the convents in Lima were so numerous that they occupied more territory than the civil population, and in 1790 in Mexico City, of the 3,387 houses, 1,985 belonged to the church, while in 1800 Humboldt estimated that the total wealth of the Mexican clergy was $100,-000,000. Most of this wealth had been obtained through the legacies of the faithful, for it had become a widespread notion that a will that did not contain a legacy in favor of the church endangered the soul of the person who made it.

Throughout the entire colonial period the Catholic church not only completely dominated religion, but also controlled all education as well. Indeed the oldest universities in the Americas were those established by the Catholics in Hispanic America, the oldest being the University of San Marcos in Lima and the university in Mexico City, both founded in 1551. Protestantism found no opportunity of gaining a foothold in Hispanic America throughout the entire colonial period. One of the factors keeping it out was the Spanish Inquisition, which was established both in Mexico and in Peru. The church was closely tied up with the state not only in colonial times but also after independence, for the wars did not alienate the people from the Catholic church; and, when the new nations formed their independent governments they, in every case, declared the Roman Catholic church the religion of the state.

Protestant work.—Protestant work in Hispanic America began in 1804, when the British and Foreign Bible Society began to publish the Bible in Portuguese. These Scriptures were distributed along the Brazilian coast by merchants and sailors as well as by colporteurs. The first Protestant church in South America was an Anglican congregation formed in Brazil to care for the religious needs of English people in Rio de Janeiro. In the 1820's Scotch colonists in Argentina and German Lutherans in Brazil organized congregations, and other immigrants from Protestant lands were permitted to form congregations. Beginning about the middle of the last century English and American missionary agencies began to plan to extend their activities to the Latin-American countries. The Presbyterians, the Southern Methodists, the Southern Baptists, and the Episcopalians have been most active in Brazil, and, as a whole, Brazil has been more hospitable to Protestantism than any of the other Latin-American countries. Important Protestant work has been established in Argentina, Chile, Paraguay, and Mexico, as well as in Peru and Bolivia. Protestant missions in Hispanic America have made a particularly important educational contribution. Mackenzie College in São Paulo, Brazil, established by the Presbyterians, has set the standards for higher education in that republic, just as Santiago College in Chile, established by the Methodists, has done much to raise educational standards for women on the west coast. These are but examples of the type of influence exerted throughout most of the republics through Protestant educational endeavor.

Even yet separation of church and state in Hispanic America has been achieved in only a few of the republics. Mexico, Brazil, Chile, and Uruguay have the largest degree of religious freedom, and their constitutions declare the Roman Catholic church no longer the religion of the state. Cuba, also, on winning independence, disestablished the church. In the other republics the Roman church is still granted special favors, and in most of them it is still the state church. Columbia, Peru, and Ecuador are the republics most dominated by Roman Catholicism and have the farthest to go in achieving religious liberty.

Canada under French control.—The story of Christianity in Canada begins with the coming of the French explorers and colonizers. Leaders like Jacques Cartier and Samuel de Champlain not only were interested in the expansion of France in the New World but were also good Catholics and to a certain extent carried their religion with them. In the process of establishing permanent French colonies along the St. Lawrence, Roman Catholicism was introduced from the start. As early as 1615, members of the Recollet order were at work in Quebec and began to carry Christian teaching to the Indians. The activity of the Recollet friars, however, yielded no permanent fruit among the savages, and in 1625 the Jesuits took over the work and thus begins one of the most heroic ventures in the history of Christian missions. The Franciscans also came to New France (1620), their center being Montreal, and both Franciscans and Jesuits pushed their Indian missions steadily westward. In the wars with the Indians that resulted from this expansion into Indian country, the missionaries and the native Christians were cruelly tortured and eventually the missions were completely destroyed.

In 1658 the first Catholic bishop, François de Laval, was appointed for Canada, and in 1674 the diocese of Quebec was created. Bishop Laval was a commanding figure in New France for many years, fighting for the rights of the church, attempting to put a stop to the liquor traffic with the Indians, as well as taking a leading part in the government. His power was co-equal with that of the governor, and he was a leading member of the sovereign council. The Catholic church became the greatest landowner in New France, controlling about one-fourth of the area allotted for settlement. Every effort was made to keep both Protestants and Protestant ideas out of the colony. The church had a monopoly on education, but the mass of the people remained illiterate. In practically every field of human activity the parish priest was the recognized leader of his flock; indeed the parish became the "backbone of French-Canadian nationality."

English rule and beginnings of Protestantism.—The first rift in the great colonial empire of France in America was made by the Treaty of Utrecht in 1713, when Newfoundland, Nova Scotia or Acadia, and the Hudson Bay country was turned over to England. Britain made attempts to Anglicize Nova Scotia by building the town of Halifax and introducing English and Scotch colonists. Many French Acadians, however, refused to take the oath of allegiance, which led to their cruel deportation. But the French Catholics who remained were allowed to exercise their religion unmolested. In the French and Indian War (1756–63) England conquered all Canada, and after 1763 all the former French colonies were a part of the British dominions. Under English rule the French Catholics were well treated, and in 1774 the famous Quebec Act granted "free exercise of religion of the Church of Rome, subject to the King's Supremacy."

The American Revolution brought a great stream of loyalist immigration into Canada from the United States which laid the foundation for the English-speaking part of British North America. By 1795 at least thirty thousand people of loyalist stock were living in Upper Canada, and their coming changed the "whole destiny of Canada." It made necessary, first of all, the establishment of English institutions, for these colonists were no less devoted to representative government than were their cousins in the United States. Their demands resulted in the passage of the Canada Act of 1791, dividing Canada into two provinces with separate governments, the English part receiving a limited amount of self-government. The rights of Catholics were once more recognized, and, to encourage Protestantism, provision was made to reserve for the support of a Protestant clergy one-seventh of all lands granted in the past or to be granted in the future for other purposes. The governor might also, with the advice of his council, erect rectories and endow them with a part of the clergy reserves.

The Loyalists naturally brought with them their religion—in fact, there were several settlements of Mennonites, Dunkers, and Quakers, as well as Presbyterians, German Reformed, German Lutherans, Anglicans, Baptists, and Methodists. Methodists, having come both from England and from the United States, were divided into several bodies, and it took six consolidations to pave the way for Methodist union in 1884. The Presbyterians likewise were divided into several different bodies, and it was not until 1875 that four distinct Presbyterian groups, each of which had been the product of previous unions, were united into one Presbyterian church in Canada.

Attempts to establish the Church of England.—As a consequence of the provisions of the Canada Act, the Church of England claimed that they alone were entitled to the clergy reserves and that the intention of the act was to create an establishment. The Presbyterians succeeded in securing a share of the clergy reserves, since their church in Scotland was an establishment, but all other Protestant bodies were shut out and their ministers were not permitted to perform marriage ceremonies. Even the Presbyterians suffered humiliating restrictions. The Anglicans also monopolized education. The injustice of this situation and the arrogant manner in which the Anglicans claimed everything for themselves aroused the "dissenters" to action and under the leadership of Adolphus Egerton Ryerson, an able Methodist leader, they united to fight for religious equality. The clergy reserves was one of the causes of the rebellion in 1837, and, with the passage of the Reunion Act of 1841, special privileges to any one religious body were doomed. Henceforth religious liberty and separation of church and state was the order of the day throughout Canada.

Expansion and church union.—With the rapid pushing westward of population the Baptists, Methodists, and Presbyterians grew rapidly, using the same frontier methods as had been found successful in the United States. As these bodies came together in the West their leaders, especially Presbyterian and Methodist, began to agitate for union. This came to fruition in the formation of the United Church of Canada in 1925, in which all the Canadian Methodists, most of the Congregationalists, and about 70 per cent of the Presbyterians merged to form a great united church. It constitutes the largest Protestant body in Canada, with more than two million adherents. The Anglican church, with 4 archbishops, 24 bishops, and 1,603,267 adherents, ranks next among Protestant bodies; while the Presbyterians with 8 synods, 47 presbyteries, and 870,000 adherents ranks third among Protestant bodies. The Baptists, with 443,341 adherents, comes fourth; and the Lutherans, with 394,194, is fifth. The Roman Catholics, with their long start over the Protestant bodies especially in the eastern provinces, has 3 Canadian archbishops, 54 bishops, and a Catholic constituency of 4,285,000.

CHAPTER VIII

CHRISTIANITY ENCIRCLES THE GLOBE

29. PERIODIC REBIRTHS OF THE MISSIONARY MOVEMENT

The term "foreign missions" refers to the expansion of Christianity beyond the confines of its own culture region and out into populations which live according to alien cultures and religions. Thus early Christianity spread out from Palestine into the Mediterranean world; and modern Christianity expands today beyond Christendom into the great non-Christian regions of the globe. Other religions also have been missionary. Buddhism, for example, has shown remarkable missionary zeal. One branch of the movement extended from India, the land of its birth, eastward through Burma and south into Siam; the other branch spread northward around Tibet and east to China and Japan. Strangely enough both Christianity and Buddhism have practically died out in the land of their birth. Had they not become missionary in spirit, they would have disappeared long ago.

Expansion and entrenchment.—The life of the church has not been uniformly expansive down through the centuries. As a rule, a period of missionary enthusiasm has been followed either by a time of religious inactivity and lukewarmness or by a period when religious energy was directed to other objectives.

Each of these periodical swings is to be accounted for by the peculiar combination of a variety of factors, religious and otherwise, which entered into each succeeding historical situation. Two of these, however, merit special mention. The great missionary movements of the church have sprung from the happy combination of a great religious awakening, on the one hand, and from an expanding geographical horizon, on the other. The one provides what might be called an area of high-pressure spiritual vitality; the other opens up avenues through which this vitality may express itself. When both of these are present, the church extends its lines; when either of them is absent, missionary zeal declines.

Even that most remarkable religious awakening which we call Pentecost was not in itself alone capable of producing a missionary movement. The church in Jerusalem and Palestine was saved from the danger of degenerating into a narrow ingrowing sect only by the fact that a certain section of the young church, as typified by Philip, Paul, and Barnabas, were aware of the fact that they were living in a world which was larger than Palestine and which by that time had come to include the whole Mediterranean area. As a result, the church set out to evangelize that area. This took centuries of preaching, planting of little churches, and martyrdom, during which time the early missionary zeal increasingly gave way to the perfecting of ecclesiastical organization, doctrinal discussions, and to other urgent tasks involved in the progressive Christianization of the area.

Later on, when the Mediterranean world had partially recovered from the devastating inroads of barbarian tribes, the surviving Mediterranean culture began to spread still farther west, north, and east, and the Europe of the Middle Ages found itself at last in the process of formation. The combination of this geographic expansion with the kindled religious fervor of the period, as manifested in the lives of individual missionaries, monastic orders, and overzealous monarchs who compelled their subjects to accept baptism, led to successive waves of missionary expansion which in time brought about the Christianization of the remaining pagan areas of Europe.

The years 1492 and 1517 are significant dates so far as the missionary history of the church is concerned. The first marks the beginning of that marvelous outreach of European political power, commerce, population, and general culture which has been one of the most striking characteristics of the last four centuries. The latter date may be taken as marking the beginning of a religious awakening which, as the Reformation, gave birth to the so-called Protestant churches and, as the Counter Reformation, quickened into new life the dormant vitality of the Roman Catholic church.

Catholic missions.—But at this point we are struck by a sharp contrast in the interest taken by the Catholic church and the Protestant churches in the welfare of the "heathen," as they were called. The shock caused by the withdrawal of northern and western Europe from the fold of the Holy Mother Church aroused that church out of its life of complaisance. New religious orders such as the Jesuits were formed for the express purpose of strengthening the church and preaching the gospel in distant lands. Long-established orders such as the Dominicans and Franciscans were seized with a new sense of mission. At the same time such Catholic powers as Spain, Portugal, and France took the lead in exploring and conquering the vast new continents beyond the sea, planting colonies which were to remain under their control for two hundred years or more. The kings and emperors of these colonial powers held themselves responsible to God for the evangelization of the heathen who had thus been delivered into their hands. Thus it is not strange that the new religious fervor of the Catholic should find an outlet in mission work. Missionaries accompanied the explorer, the conqueror, and the pioneer tradesman wherever they went. Francis Xavier (1506–52) carried his gospel message as far east as Japan. The Franciscans began work among the Indians of Quebec in 1615. Las Casas labored to protect the South American Indians from the greed of European conquerors. The sword and the cross were partners in a thrilling undertaking. By the year 1622 the Congregation of Propaganda was established in Rome, which has since functioned as the great co-ordinating missionary agency of the Catholic church.

Protestant missions.—At first thought it seems strange that for two hundred years after the Reformation the Protestant churches, aside from a few isolated voices, manifested almost no concern over the condition of the heathen world. Yet there were reasons for this. Their time and attention were occupied with urgent matters nearer home. They had to entrench themselves in their own countries, lest the reform movement be snuffed out in its infancy by hostile powers, both ecclesiastical and political. Theological differences had to be thrashed out; creeds had to be written; new church organizations devised and set up; the Scriptures had to be translated and circulated. In due time the early religious fervor of Reformation days cooled down into a life of religious formalism, worldliness, and skepticism. Furthermore, the Protestant nations such as Denmark, Britain, and Holland, had not as yet really begun to expand as great colonial and commercial powers, which might offer both soil and protection for missionary work.

The spiritual awakening which eventually gave birth to the modern missionary enterprise of the Protestant churches dates from the spontaneous outbreak of religious fervor among the Pietists of Germany in the seventeenth and eighteenth centuries. This awakening spread over into Britain in the Wesleyan revival and later into North America itself, where a series of frontier revivals strengthened the church and made it increasingly sensitive to its evangelistic obligations both at home and abroad.

It so happened that this spiritual awakening coincided in a general way with the rise of Britain, Holland, and Denmark as great colonial powers. The earlier interest in international commerce, as carried on by the British East India Company and by the Dutch East India Company, was greatly intensified with the coming of the Industrial Revolution with its mass production, its improved means of communication, and its growing need for raw materials and expanding markets. Little by little trading posts developed into colonial empires. Thus inevitably the attention of Protestant countries began to turn to wider horizons. It is not strange, then, that religious interest should at last be turned in the same direction.

As early as 1701 the Society for the Propagation of the Gospel in Foreign Parts had been organized within the Church of England. On the Continent the response of the king of Denmark to the missionary zeal of German Pietists led to the beginning of the work of the Danish-Halle Mission in India. Under Count Zinzendorf the Moravians caught the missionary spirit and before long set the pace for missionary work, which in proportion of foreign missionaries to the membership of the supporting church at home has not been equaled by any other body.

In the meantime, some of the colonists along the Atlantic seaboard had begun to manifest an interest in the welfare of the American Indian. For example, John Eliot (1604–90) labored for forty years among the Indians of Massachusetts, translating the Scriptures and gathering his converts into Christian settlements where they might the better be weaned away from their pagan customs. David Brainard (1718–47) burned his life out prematurely among the aborigines of the Delaware region, but his memory became an inspiration to others to follow in similar self-forgetting devotion.

Modern missions.—The above may be considered as experimental and preparatory efforts. It is generally agreed that the real beginnings of the modern missionary movement among Protestant churches dates from 1792, when a little group of English Baptists banded themselves together into a missionary society to send William Carey to the foreign field. There are three main reasons for this opinion. First, because from now on the missionary enterprise was characterized by a new sense of individual responsibility on the part of an increasing number of Christians and by the development of strong and permanent missionary societies for the support of regular bands of workers abroad. Second, by this time the home base, which heretofore had been confined to a few countries in western Europe, was in process of expansion into a vast Christendom including North America, South Africa, Australia, and New Zealand, where rapidly growing resources of men and money made possible the remarkable missionary growth of the nineteenth century. Third, the next twenty or thirty years witnessed the founding of almost all the great missionary societies which have since been the mainstay of the missionary enterprise.

Among the many motives which have inspired the sacrifices necessary to sustain this movement may be mentioned the natural impulse of the human heart to share with others the Christian experience of deliverance from sin and the awakening to a new life; obedience to the command of the Great Commission; gratitude to Christ and love to Christ; humanitarian sympathies and pity for those in distress; the desire to extend the Kingdom of Heaven which brings not only glory to God but also personal satisfaction to every member of that Kingdom; and the growing sense of human solidarity and an awakening to the fact that from now on the whole of humanity will rise or fall together. The Christian has long believed that before God he is his brother's keeper; but to an increasing degree our brother across the water is becoming our keeper. Mission work seeks to make him and us better brothers.

30. THE CHRISTIAN MOVEMENT PENETRATES INDIA AND AFRICA

India.—The Christian religion first reached India sometime during the first five centuries of the Christian Era. Some of the results of this early evangelism still survive in a small group known as "Syrian Christians" in South India. Catholic missionaries accompanied the early Portuguese traders, and as early as 1543 a bishopric was established at Goa on the west coast. At present the Catholics constitute about two-fifths of the total Christian community. Brief reference has already been made to the preparatory work of the Danish-Halle Mission.

The real beginnings of Protestant missionary work in India are associated with the names of two or three outstanding missionaries belonging to various societies. William Carey labored in India from 1793 to 1834. He and his companions represented the British Baptists and devoted most of their time and energy to translation work, publication of literature, preaching, and the establishing of a college and seminary at Serampore, which still survives. John Scudder was the first medical missionary. He labored in South India from 1819 to 1855 as the missionary of the Reformed church in America. Alexander Duff was the first missionary from Scotland and a pioneer in the work of educational missions, introducing the policy of making English the medium of higher education and seeking to train his students in European culture as well as in the Christian religion, to the neglect of the best in their own venerable civilization—a policy which later was abandoned.

Each large missionary area presents certain features which are characteristic and which place their own peculiar stamp upon the course of the Christian enterprise in that land. Four of these may be mentioned in connection with the work in India: the caste system with its rigid stratification of society; the highly diversified forms of religion, as presented by Hinduism and Mohammedanism, designed to meet an equally diversified range in the interpretation of religious need; the political control of the country by a "Christian nation" of the West, together with the growing agitation for autonomy; and the extreme ignorance and poverty of the masses. Each of these has exerted a powerful influence upon Christian activities.

Because of the satisfaction of the upper castes with their own position and philosophy of life and because of the extreme need of the lower masses, in India as in no other country mission work has been directed to the alleviation of the low castes and the outcastes. Their ignorance and degradation have enormously intensified the problem of bringing about individual regeneration and Christian nurture, of establishing a self-supporting native church, and of improving the general social and economic conditions under which they must live. Sometimes the improvement seems very small. The main promise today lies in the talented native leadership which is slowly emerging as a result of decades of patient toil.

Almost from the beginning special emphasis has been laid upon educational work, to meet the almost complete illiteracy of the submerged masses. The government (British) was glad to co-operate by providing liberal financial assistance. As a result of this, the various missions have been able to build up and maintain an exceptionally imposing array of schools, ranging from the kindergarten up to the well-equipped college, all closely co-ordinated with the governmental systems. How long this state support will continue as political authority passes more and more into Indian hands, or what the conditions will be, the future alone will reveal.

The traditional seclusion of the higher-class women in zenanas, the general ignorance and backwardness of the outcaste women, the prevailing customs governing child marriage, and the servile position of widows have all led to special emphasis being given to work among women. It was largely to meet this challenge that women's missionary societies were first of all organized in the West, and an exceptionally large number of woman missionaries have found their way to

India. No country rises much above the general level of its womanhood.

One of the characteristic features of the work in India has been the recurrent mass movements. By culture and training the Indian is not an individualist. Caste discipline is extremely strict against any recalcitrant individual. Consequently, one is more inclined to move as a member of a caste or of a local community than as an individual. Thus it happens that since the days of the Telugu revival under John E. Clough in 1878, when six thousand coolies were baptized within six weeks, there has been an increasing tendency for whole communities of outcaste or low-caste people to seek admission into the church under the guidance of their own native leadership. In recent years, and especially in view of the declining support coming from the West, the providing of proper training and pastoral oversight for these thousands who present themselves at the door of the church has severely taxed the resources of the Christian forces. The future status and power of the church in India depends largely upon the degree of enlightenment and sanctity which these mass-movement converts may be able to acquire in the next few years.

Africa south of the desert.—Although the Mediterranean coast of Africa had been one of the strongholds of the Christian faith during the first four or five centuries of our era, a series of reverses culminating in conquest by the Moslems had virtually obliterated the Christian church, with the exception of the Copts in Egypt and the closely related Abyssinian church in

Ethiopia. For some reason early Christianity had failed to root itself farther south in equatorial Africa.

To the Dominicans, the Jesuits, and the Moravians belongs the honor of planting the first missionary stations on the fringe of the great unknown continent, following the voyages of the Portuguese explorers; but by the opening of the nineteenth century few permanent results remained of these pioneer efforts.

Africa south of the Equator presented its own characteristic features which have been the chief influences in molding the missionary enterprise during the last hundred years: the extreme difficulty in penetrating into the interior of the country; malaria and other tropical diseases which won for Africa the reputation of being "the white man's graveyard"; three or four hundred years of shameless exploitation of a backward population by the greed of Europeans and Americans, resulting first of all in the slave trade and later in various types of forced labor in order that the white man's industries might flourish; the partitioning and repartitioning of the continent into a score of colonies, big and little; the general disintegration of tribal life and of the controls of social custom before the rapid inrush of the white man's civilization; the alarming advance of Mohammedan propaganda in most of the area just south of the Sahara Desert, preaching and practicing racial equality within the fellowship of the faithful in contrast to class and race distinctions insisted upon by Europeans; rivalry between Catholic and Protestant missions; and finally difficulties experienced in coming to terms with colonial authorities some of whose policies were open to severe condemnation.

Although some American societies have been maintaining mission work in Africa for many years, most of the work is carried on by English, Scottish, and Continental societies. Little by little the missionaries pushed their way into the interior, by demonstrating their genuine interest in and value to the African. Thus hostile chiefs and tribes were gradually won over until today the Christian movement gives every appearance of being permanently rooted in the continent. As a rule, the earlier missionaries occupied themselves not only in preaching the gospel but also in reducing the language of illiterate tribes to writing and then in translating the Bible into these tongues. David Livingstone stands out as the most illustrious of the missionary explorers. Joining the Moffats in South Africa in 1840, he married their daughter and spent the first few years in routine missionary service among neighboring tribes. But he soon became convinced that the best way to combat the scourge of Africa, the slave traffic, and to extend the Kingdom of God in so vast a continent was to penetrate its unknown jungles and open it up to the gaze and better influences of the outside world. After twenty years spent in such pioneer work, he was found dead upon his knees in a native hut in central Africa. But today Africa is no longer an unknown land.

Africa has been the scene of a number of experiments in what is known as industrial missions, designed to teach the people more efficient methods in farming and in other industries, and thus to raise their standards of living. Some of these experiments have proven disappointing here as elsewhere, but others such as the Lovedale Institute in South Africa have done for this continent what Hampton or Tuskegee have done for the Negro in America.

Of necessity medical work has long been carried on by many societies. Conditions demanded it. Of recent years the most illustrious missionary in Africa has been Albert Schweitzer, a representative of the Paris Evangelical Mission located at Lambarene in the French Congo. The fact that a man who had made such a name for himself as a musician, a philosopher, and a biblical scholar should take up medicine and give himself to the needy people of Africa has made a profound impression upon the whole Christian world.

Perhaps the most thrilling example of missionary progress in Africa is the story of the work of the Church Missionary Society in Uganda. This secluded country, called to the attention of the outside world by Henry M. Stanley, soon became the unhappy scene of political and religious rivalry between the British, the French, and the Moslems. Eventually British influence became dominant, and, with it, Protestant work gained a secure foothold in the country. In the meantime, as early as 1876 a band of eight enthusisatic young missionaries set out from England to evangelize this land. Within a year their number was reduced to three; and in two years' time Mackay of Uganda was the only survivor left. For twelve years he labored on against terrible odds. The story of his career—his early struggles and later successes, the wise use of his engineering skill, his keen diplomacy, his tireless energy, his supreme sacrifice for the people he loved—all this reads like a romance. He was finally driven from his field through the intrigues of Arabs and forced to take refuge at the southern end of Lake Victoria Nyanza, where he died three years later, in 1890. But the work thus begun has continued to prosper. The church today is largely self-directing and self-supporting. The cathedral at Kampala, dedicated in 1919, is probably the largest Christian edifice in Africa.

Today the most critical question facing Christian people is the adjustment of race relationships in South Africa, where conflict between the white and powerful minority and the black majority has long been a burning issue.

31. THE CHRISTIAN MOVEMENT PENETRATES CHINA AND JAPAN

China.—No more remarkable evidence of the expansive power of the early church can be found than the fact that by the sixth or seventh century, while Christianity was being introduced for the second time into Britain, Christian missionaries of the Nestorian church had worked their way as far east as Sianfu, in northwestern China. Here a Christian community seems to have survived until the end of the thirteenth century. The Catholic form of Christianity reached China about 1300, following the visit of Marco Polo; but after a hundred years of precarious existence it disappeared, only to be revived again about 1580 by the arrival in southern China of Ricci and his companions, who eventually worked their way as far north as Peking. Once again governmental favor was squandered away by political intrigue on the part of the missionaries and by ecclesiastical disputes, resulting in the banishment of the missionaries in 1724. But it was impossible to eradicate entirely the Catholic church; and, with the coming of more favorable conditions during the nineteenth century, it has continued to root itself still more deeply in the country.

Protestant work began with the coming of Robert Morrison, the pioneer missionary of the London Missionary Society, who labored in Canton and Macao from 1807 to 1834, translating the Bible, publishing a Chinese dictionary and grammar, and preaching the gospel as best he could—but with most discouraging results. In 1829 the American Board sent out its first missionaries, Bridgman and Abeel. In 1834 Peter Parker established a hospital in Canton, the first institution of the kind in the Far East.

Since 1834 the course of Christian missions has been molded by the following conditions. First, by the fact that the closed door of China was opened only as a result of successive defeats in war. This meant that the introduction of Christianity was associated with the humiliation of defeat and the imposition of the opium traffic. Second, China herself rightly boasted of a long and honorable history and of a venerable culture consisting of a well-regulated social organization, artistic accomplishments, and of a vast literature. Consequently, she felt little need of any contribution from the "barbarians" of the West. Third, the three prevailing religions—Taoism, Buddhism, and Confucianism—although lacking in their original vitality, still ministered fairly well to the religious needs of the people as these were understood. Fourth, beginning with the revolution of 1911, China began to pass through the most remarkable transformation ever attempted by four hundred million people—a revolution that at the same time was political, educational, social, economic, and religious. Fifth, the coming of communism with its Marxian philosophy of life, and more recently still the invasion by Japan with its ambitions to "Japanize" the Far East according to the will of heaven, is fast turning China into a battleground between three rival philosophies—communism, Mikadoism, and Christian democracy.

Under such conditions it is not strange that Christian growth should have been exceedingly slow during the nineteenth century. By the end of the century, the Christian community did not exceed one hundred thousand, and even this was cruelly decimated in the persecutions attending the Boxer outbreak. This, along with the Chinese esteem for learning, accounts for the fact that more and more emphasis was laid upon educational work, until the time came when the most outstanding institutions were mission schools and colleges, which along with Christian hospitals served as models for governmental institutions founded later on. As a result of this educational policy, a large proportion of the leaders of the awakening China were either professing Christians or were educated in Christian schools. There have also arisen a considerable number of exceptionally talented Christian leaders who as educators, as pastors, and as administrators have shared with the missionaries the prosecution of the work.

Certain features of church life deserve special mention. The Chinese church has been highly evangelical and has repeatedly launched great campaigns for the winning of converts on a nation-wide scale. The China Inland Mission has devoted itself especially to carrying the gospel message to the remote regions of the interior. Since the turn of the century, and in spite of occasional antiforeign sentiment, the Chinese have been more favorably disposed to the work of the missionaries, and as a result the Christian movement has spread like a network over the whole land.

At the same time this evangelistic zeal has been supplemented more recently by attention given to "religious education" and training for the development of Christian character and efficiency in religious activities. Face to face with the task of reaching four hundred million people with the gospel, the Christian forces in China have pushed forward along the lines of Christian co-operation especially in educational work, in actual church union (the Church of Christ in China), and in building up a strong and efficient National Christian Council. Unfortunately, this trend toward a wider Christian fellowship has been marred by a split between conservatives and liberals, which so far shows little promise of healing.

Within the last few years the work of both schools

and churches has been seriously disturbed in the regions occupied by the Japanese invasion. The future is uncertain and obscure. On the other hand, the courageous ministrations of Christian workers, native and foreign, to Chinese victims and refugees have done much to win the gratitude of the Chinese people. Even if the Western powers have been slow to come to their rescue, they feel that the Christian church has stood by them in their hour of need.

Japan.—The first Christian missionary, Francis Xavier, reached Japan in 1549. Although his own sojourn in the islands lasted only two and a half years, he was followed by other missionaries; and by the year 1581 the Catholics could boast of a hundred and fifty thousand communicants. The Christian cause enjoyed a remarkable growth for some fifty years. Eventually, however, political wire-pulling on the part of Catholic clergy, rivalry between the Catholic orders themselves, and the opposition of Japanese religious leaders brought on severe persecutions, and the whole community was snuffed out to such an extent that only a few traces survived until the reopening of the country to foreigners in the middle of the last century.

Within ten years after the signing of the treaty opening a few seaports to the residence of foreigners (1858), eight Protestant societies had already established themselves, and ever since then mission work in Japan has been predominantly American. As in the case of the other countries already studied, the early missionaries proved to be men of exceptional intelligence and resourcefulness, ready to make the best of any opportunity which presented itself. Hepburn of the American Board gave himself to medical work and to translating the Scriptures; Brown of the Dutch Reformed church opened the first school in Japan at Yokohama; Verbeck of the Reformed church was perhaps the greatest of them all. As educator, evangelist, translator, and counselor to the Japanese authorities he profoundly influenced the period of national awakening.

Here again the course of Christian missions has been molded by local conditions. From time to time the attitude of the country has swung from one of extreme hospitality to things foreign over to an equally extreme devotion to things Japanese, with corresponding suspicion of foreigners and their influence. No other oriental country has so highly esteemed universal education or raised its people to such a high percentage of literacy. No other country of the East has so successfully succeeded in supplementing the traditional agricultural economy of the country by adopting the latest forms of Western industrialism, with all its attendant increase in wealth and effectiveness and also in evils resulting from well-known forms of exploitation. No other country has been so fired with pride of race and of divine origin and with a consciousness of a commission from the gods to dominate the East—if not the whole world.

In response to such conditions as these, the Christian church in Japan presents its own peculiar features. In contrast to India and even China, a considerable portion of the first converts belonged to the upper middle classes who occupied respectable positions economically, intellectually, and socially. As a result, the Christian movement has until recently been largely confined to the urban centers to the neglect of rural districts and peasant population. This is now being remedied largely through the leadership of Kagawa. Kagawa's self-sacrificing devotion to the underprivileged masses and his rare combination of practical efficiency with deep mystical piety have made his life an inspiration to his Christian brethren in all lands.

Because of the type of membership, the native churches have been in a better position to assume self-support and self-direction than has been the case in other countries. Almost from the beginning educated and talented native leadership arose capable of working side by side with the missionary. Consequently, the church in Japan has gone farther than any other mission church in achieving a full degree of local autonomy and in determining general policies from year to year—policies with which the Christian worker, both foreign and native, comply.

The ample provision made by the government both for universal education and for medical service has made it unnecessary for the church to promote such activities, aside from kindergarten work, a few excellent colleges, and one or two hospitals. The major stress has rather been laid upon evangelistic work, founding and maintaining local churches, and carrying on social service work on behalf of orphans, prisoners, and against prostitution and intemperance. One distinctive feature has been "newspaper evangelism," through the use of the local press for the dissemination of the Christian message.

In Japan, as in no other mission country, the church has been compelled to face the question of God or Caesar, made doubly difficult by the claims of divine origin and authority of the Mikado. Christians are repeatedly called upon to face such delicate questions as these: To what extent can Christian schools participate in the official Shinto rites which are demanded of all educational institutions? What should be the attitude of a Christian to Japanese imperial aggression in China or elsewhere? To what extent can the Christian churches submit to governmental regulations imposed upon all religious bodies in Japan and Korea, without seriously forfeiting their right to self-control and their prime obligation to God rather than man? As in Germany, so in Japan and Korea, the question of church and state has assumed an urgency which we of America scarcely realize.

32. MISSIONARY ORGANIZATION AND OPERATION

The aims of the foreign missionary enterprise have been expressed in a variety of ways according to doctrinal differences and changing conditions. But, in general, Christian people have sought thereby to share the blessings they have experienced through Jesus Christ with those of other lands who have not been so favored.

Organization and methods.—For the carrying-out of this purpose there have been developed both efficient organizations and effective methods of work. The first societies in Britain, Germany, or America were voluntary associations of missionary enthusiasts who pooled their prayers and their gifts to support the enterprise abroad. But gradually these pioneer societies became transformed into denominational boards, through which the denomination as such sought to carry out the missionary obligations of which it was becoming increasingly aware. These boards, backed up by the denominational constituency, provide the unfailing fund of resources which give strength and continuity to the work.

Following the example of Paul, the first effort in each case was to establish the work in strategic centers of importance. The Christian cause thus rooted itself in foreign soil, and then proceeded to spread out after the manner of a strawberry plant, sending out its "runners" into the surrounding territory where they proceeded to root themselves as mission stations, and these in turn spread out again to take root as out-stations. Thus little by little vast areas have been covered with Christian centers given to preaching, educational work, medical service, and other forms of Christian activity.

In due time the weakness and defects of strictly denominational organizations became apparent both at home and abroad. The task proved too big and too complicated for any one body. Accordingly there has been a growing tendency to seek closer co-operation. At the home base this has given rise to the Foreign Missions Conference, which meets yearly for the purpose of co-ordinating the activities of the boards located in America. The International Missionary Council is the more inclusive body through which the boards of Europe and America and the mission churches of all lands take counsel with one another and engage in a limited amount of concerted action. As symbolic of this trend must also be mentioned the long series of international missionary conferences, especially those held in Jerusalem in 1928 and in Madras in 1938, in which an increasingly prominent place has been given to the so-called "younger" churches in the total enterprise.

Of recent years Christians have come to appreciate as never before the indispensable place which the church, both as a local congregation and as a wider fellowship, must occupy in the ongoing movement which we call the cause of Christ. Among the many efforts made to strengthen the church on the foreign field have been promising experiments in church union in India, China, Japan, and the Philippines. When two or three denominational bodies, none of which is numerous, are thus united, a new sense of strength is created in the midst of a surrounding society that is none too friendly. In all the major mission fields National Christian Councils have bound together the foreign "missions" and the native churches in mutual consultation and the administration of their common interests. From now on much more thought must be given to strengthening the church under competent leadership if the Christian movement is to be assured of continued growth and influence in the world.

Objections and defects.—The missionary enterprise has

always been carried on in the face of opposition at home. "If God wants to save the heathen, he will save them without our help"; "We have enough to do at home"; "Other religions are good enough"; "Too much money goes to overhead"; etc. The missionary cause has survived such attacks as these; but it would be partisan blindness to fail to recognize that defects which must be remedied are constantly manifesting themselves. Some of these may be mentioned, for the cause of missions has at last passed from the romantic stage to one of calmer appraisal. In some cases over-zealous propaganda has accentuated the processes of disintegration in certain localities to an alarming degree. In our effort to give the best we had, we have sometimes established our mission institutions on an economic and cultural level too high above the immediate attainment of the people. By virtue of the type of education offered in mission schools, too large a proportion of the graduates have sought their life-work in other and more lucrative channels rather than in ministering to the churches and communities from which they came. All too frequently the Christian forces abroad have been restrained from making the necessary adjustment to changing conditions because of opposition on the part of the supporting churches at home arising out of attitudes that are out of date and lamentable ignorance. It is tragic when the cause which we support with our prayers and our gifts is halted and hobbled by our own attitudes which are fifty years behind the times.

Accomplishments.—On the other hand, this cataloguing of shortcomings should be balanced by a recognition of the services rendered in many lands. Especially during the first few decades, the missionaries have been pioneers in a variety of humanitarian services which heretofore had been almost entirely neglected; such as educational and medical work, the emancipation of women, improvement of rural conditions, and in combatting some of the more glaring vices such as foot-binding, opium traffic, prostitution, child marriage, etc. Later on high-minded native leaders have themselves undertaken these reforms; but the missionary was the first in setting the leaven to work. Although the presence of the missionary has sometimes been the occasion of riots and has been used by Western governments as the pretext for demanding greater political and economic concessions, nevertheless on the whole the missionaries have been agents of international good will. They have served as living examples of the best features of our Western culture and religion. Through their letters and their periodical return to the homeland, they have done more than any other agency to kindle an interest in other peoples and in their welfare.

The competition of the Christian movement has served to arouse the indigenous religions out of centuries of lethargy and to set a new ferment of reform to working in their midst. This reviving of pagan religions is the last thing that some supporters of missions would desire. But those who are primarily concerned with the welfare of people will rejoice in these reforms. Not all non-Christians will be converted to the Christian faith—at least not for a long time. Those who remain true to their old loyalties will only stand to profit by any reform which takes place.

Even after governments and other agencies have taken over many of the so-called secondary activities, such as educational, medical, and social service work, there will still remain that most distinctive service of the church which we call "spiritual." This is the most precious blessing which Christianity has brought in the past; it will continue to be so in the future. Year after year thousands of people the world over have been born into a newness of life through the preaching and living of the gospel message. The slaves of sin have been liberated; the depressed and discouraged are inspired by new hope; those who are wandering in mental confusion have found a new meaning and purpose through accepting some form of the Christian interpretation of life. So long as the world endures, each generation of mankind everywhere will stand in need of some orientation to life and its meaning; and so long as the church can really meet this need effectively, there will be an undiminishing call for her services.

The challenge of the future.—After a hundred and fifty years the expanding church looks back not only at a past full of accomplishments but also at a present and a future full of challenges; with their attendant problems. In any dynamic movement the solving of one problem raises another which must be met. We are still wrestling with the adjustment of relationships between mission boards and mission churches, and this will continue until the churches have passed out of the age of adolescence into maturity. Every field presents its own problem of how best to bring about a greater degree of co-operation and even organic union, while preserving the necessary amount of diversity in doctrine and practice. Closely akin to this is the difficulty in preserving the unity of the church from the threatened split between conservatives and liberals. Liberals and conservatives must learn to live and work together, even on the foreign field. There remains the task of entering areas still almost entirely neglected, such as certain secluded corners of the globe, and certain types of population, such as the peasants and fisherfolk of Japan.

One of the most urgent questions at the present time is that of preserving the liberty to teach and preach and of adjusting the rival claims of Caesar and of God. Again, how shall the Christian religion, with its claims to be the one supreme channel of divine grace, be related to other religions which cannot in all honesty be waved aside as utterly false and useless? How can the church abroad be further strengthened in numbers, economic resources, intelligent experience, and unfailing devotion that it may prove worthy of the charge committed to it? This is matched by a corresponding problem of strengthening the church at the home base, keeping alive the flame of missionary enthusiasm which must not be allowed to die down prematurely, even in days of financial depression.

Enfin, the whole world today, and especially the newly awakened countries of the East, present a vast battleground—the scene of a life-and-death struggle between four great rivals for world-supremacy: communism, naziism, mikadoism, and Christianity, especially as the latter is associated with democracy. Each of these claims to be founded on and sanctioned by God, or at least some Ultimate Reality. Each one boasts of providing the one way of salvation which alone will set the world right. The fate of mankind for the next few decades or centuries hangs in the balance. Certainly the church of today does not lack a challenge worthy of calling forth again the fidelity of the martyrs and the untiring zeal and devotion of the apostles.

We have traced in briefest outline the history of the church for nineteen hundred years. It presents the appearance of a mighty gulf stream, emerging from the narrow confines of Palestine, flowing down through history and out into the world, and bathing distant lands in the quickening warmth of its spiritual vitality. From century to century the inner quality of this movement—its power and its weakness, its purity and its corruption—has depended upon the quality of life of each successive generation of professing Christians. This is true of the present generation. It will remain true of the future.

BIBLIOGRAPHY

BAKER, A. G. *Christian Missions and a New World Culture.* Chicago: Willett, Clark & Co., 1934.

BEVAN, E. *Christianity.* "Home University Library of Modern Knowledge." New York: Henry Holt & Co., 1932.

BINNS, L. E. *The Reformation in England.* London: Duckworth, 1937.

CASE, S. J. *Makers of Christianity,* Vol. I: *From Jesus to Charlemagne.* New York: Henry Holt & Co., 1934.

DEANESLY, M. *A History of the Medieval Church, 590–1500.* London: Methuen & Co., Ltd., 1925.

DUNCAN-JONES, C. M. *An Outline of Church History from the Acts of the Apostles to the Reformation.* 3 vols. London: George Allen & Unwin, 1938.

GARRISON, W. E. *The March of Faith.* New York: Harper & Bros., 1933.

KIDD, B. J. *The Churches of Eastern Christendom.* London: Faith Press, 1927.

LATOURETTE, K. S. *A History of the Expansion of Christianity.* 3 vols. New York: Harper & Bros., 1937–39.

————. *Missions Tomorrow.* New York: Harper & Bros., 1936.

MACKINNON, J. *The Origins of the Reformation.* New York: Longmans, Green & Co., 1939.

McNEILL, J. T. *Makers of Christianity,* Vol. II: *From Alfred the Great to Schleiermacher.* New York: Henry Holt & Co., 1935. (Out of print.)

McNEILL, J. T.; SPINKA, M.; and WILLOUGHBY, H. R. *Environmental Factors in Christian History.* Chicago: University of Chicago Press, 1939.

MECHAM, J. L. *Church and State in Latin America.* Chapel Hill: University of North Carolina Press, 1934.

MOEHLMAN, C. H. *The Story of Christianity in Outline.* Rochester: Colgate-Rochester Divinity School, 1930.

OLIVER, E. H. *The Winning of the Frontier*. Toronto: United Church Publishing House, 1930.

ROWE, H. K. *History of the Christian People*. New York: Macmillan Co., 1931.

SPINKA, M. *Christianity Confronts Communism*. New York: Harper & Bros., 1936.

SWEET, W. W. *The Story of Religion in America*. 2d ed. New York: Harper & Bros., 1939.

――――. *Makers of Christianity*, Vol. III: *From John Cotton to Lyman Abbot*. New York: Henry Holt & Co., 1937.

WAND, J. W. C. *A History of the Early Church to A.D. 500*. London: Methuen & Co., Ltd., 1937.

――――. *A History of the Modern Church from 1500 to the Present Day*. New York: Thomas Crowell Co., 1930.

ZERNOV, N. *Moscow, the Third Rome*. New York: Macmillan Co., 1937. (A brief survey of the Russian church.)

INDEX

Abailard, Peter, 91
Absolutism, political, 176 ff.
Acontius, Jacob, 132
Acts, Book of, 11
Adelard of Bath, 91
Adrian IV, pope, 79
Africa, 246
African Methodist Episcopal Church, 218
African Methodist Zion Church, 218
Aidan, 63
Alaric, 49
Albania, church of, 166
Alcuin, 69, 72 ff.
Alexander, bishop of Alexandria, 35
Alexander I of Russia, 189
Alexander III, pope, 80
Alexandria, 3, 29, 31, 35, 37–38; patriarchate of, 162, 164
Alexius I, emperor, 144
Alexius IV, emperor, 146
Alexius Michaelovich, Russian czar, 156
Alfred the Great, 74
Ambrose, 40–41, 51
American Bible Society, 215
American churches sever Old World connections, 209–10
American Revolution, 233
American Sunday School Union, 215
American Tract Society, 215
Anabaptists, 127 ff., 169
Anglicanism. *See* Church of England

Anglo-Saxons, 49, 58, 59, 62 ff.
Anselm, archbishop of Canterbury, 79, 92
Anti-Catholic movements, 215, 219
Antioch, 9, 10, 19, 23, 37, 145; partriarchate of, 136, 137, 165, 167
Antony, 43, 46
Apologists, 19 ff., 30
Apostles, 10, 15
Apostles' Creed, 15, 31
Arabs, 137, 165
Arat scholars, 91
Architecture, 97
Arians, 36–37, 45, 53, 54
Aristotle, 91 ff.
Arius, 35 f.
Arles, Council of (314), 35, 58
Armenian church, 167
Arminianism, Arminius, 170, 174
Arnulf of Metz, 67
Arnulfing or Carolingian house, 67 ff.
Articles, Anglican, 121, 123
Asbury, Francis, 212
Ascetic orders, in Counter Reformation, 132 f.
Asceticism, 28, 41 ff., 60 ff., 83 ff., 101
Athanasius, 36–37, 46
Augustana (Swedish) Synod, 219
Augustine of Canterbury, 62–63
Augustine of Hippo, 51–52, 69 f.
Augustus, 1, 2
Aurelian, 23

Baldwin, Count, of Edessa, 145
Balkans, 138, 139, 140, 149, 165
Baptism, infant, 27
Baptist colleges, 214
Baptist revival, 207
Baptists, 169, 175; Canadian, 234, 235; in Colonial America, 205; English, 205; on the frontier, 211–12; following American independence, 209; and the Revolution, 208
Barnabas, 10–11
Barth, Karl, 224
Basel, Council of, 149
Basil of Caesarea, 44–45, 48–49
Batu, 153
Baxter, Richard, 185
Beaton, David, 124
Becket, Thomas, 80
Bede, the Venerable, 64–65, 72
Belgic Confession, 116
Bellarmine, 178
Benedict of Aniane, 84
Benedict of Nursia, 48–49, 84
Benedictine *Rule*, 48–49, 64
Berdyaev, Nicholas, 159
Bergius, John, 183
Bernard of Clairvaux, 86
Bible: in English, 118 f., 120; in German, 104; in Latin, 134
Bishop of London, the, 201
Bishops, 15–16, 22, 25, 40–41, 47, 52
Bismarck, 193
Boethius, 54, 73
Bohemond, 145
Bolshevist party, 160
Boniface, 65, 68, 70, 82
Book of Discipline, Scottish, 125
Boris, czar of Bulgaria, 139
Bossuet, 183
Boxer outbreak, 252
Brainard, David, 241

Brethren of the common life, 88, 97
British East India Company, 240
Britons (British), 57, 62
Brown, 255
Bruno, Giordano, 181
Bucer, Martin, 107 f., 112, 121
Buddhism, 236, 252
Bulgaria, 139, 152, 153, 166
Bullinger, Henry, 111, 130
Bunyan, John, 185
Burgundians, 53, 54
Byzantine church, 135, 137, 138, 139, 140, 144, 150, 162
Byzantine Empire, 137, 140, 141, 143, 144, 145, 147, 148, 150, 154, 155

California, Catholic missions in, 228
Calixtus, George, 183
Callistus, bishop, 28
Calvin, John, 111 ff., 122, 130
Calvinism, 114 ff.
Cambridge Platform, first Congregational book of discipline, 202
Camp meeting, 214
Campbell, Alexander, 211
Campbell, Thomas, 211
Canada, 231–35; English rule in, 232–34; English and Scotch immigration to, 232–33
Canada Act, 233
Canadian churches, membership of, 235
Canon law, 76
Capetian kings of France, 75
Capitalism, 100, 117, 181
Captivity, papal, 82
Carey, William, 242, 243
Carroll, John, first Catholic bishop, 210

Cartier, Jacques, 231

Cassian, John, 47, 48

Cassiodorus, 47–48, 54

Castellio, Sebastian, 132

Catechism, Roman, 134

Catechumenate, 31

Catherine of Aragon, 119, 122

Catholic missions, 238, 250, 254

Catholic revival, 189–90

Catholicism, in colonial Hispanic America, 226–30

Catholics, 206, 220

Celibacy, clerical, 77

Celts, races of, 57, 59; Christianity of, 59 ff.

Central America, colonization of, 226

Chalcedon, Council of (451), 38, 135, 136, 137

Challenge of the future, 262

Champlain, Samuel de, 231

Charlemagne (Karl the Great), 68 ff., 76, 84, 142; reforms of, 69 ff.

Charles of Anjou, 148

Charles V, emperor, 102, 104, 106

Charles Martel, 68

China, 250; Nestorianism in, 138

China Inland Mission, 253

Christian democracy, 252

Christian Socialism, 194–95

Christian unity, movements toward, 182–83, 197–98

Chrodegang of Metz, 70 f.

Chrysostom, John, 41

Church of Christ in China, 253

"Church in the Desert," 179–80

Church of England, 170, 174–76, 185, 194; in the colonies, 199–201, 234

Church in Japan, 255

Church union, 224–25; in Canada, 235; promotion of worldwide, 226

Cistercians, 85 f.

Civil War, the, 217, 218

Clairmont, 144

Clement of Alexandria, 29, 31

Clement VII, pope, 106, 119

Clergy reserves, 234–35

Clough, John E., 246

Clovis, 54–55

Cluny, reform of, 84 ff.

Colet, John, 96, 118

College of Cardinals, 77

College of New Jersey (Princeton), 204, 208, 209

Colleges: church, 214; Congregational, 202; Methodist, 214, 221

Colonial churches, Old World connections of, 206–7

Colored Baptists, 218

Colored Methodist Episcopal, 218

Columba, 61

Columbanus, 83

Commerce, 100

Communism, 252

Conciliarism, 82 f., 102, 104 f., 125

Concordat of Worms, 79

Confucianism, 252

Congregation of Propaganda, 239

Congregational churches, first formed, 202

Congregational colleges, 214

Congregational ministers: political influence of, 201, 202; and the Revolution, 208

Congregationalists, Canadian, 235

Congregationalism: Colonial 201–3; on the frontier, 213; after independence, 209; and revivalism, 214; and the Revolution, 208

Congregations, Presbyterian, at end of Colonial period, 204

Connecticut, 203; Congregationalism in, 203
Constantine, 33 ff., 38, 40, 50, 141
Constantine XI, emperor, 150
Constantinople, 34; Council of, 37, 140, 141, 146, 147, 148, 149, 150; patriarchate of, 135, 137, 152, 154, 162, 163, 164, 166
Contemplative life, 88, 131
Copernicus, Nicholas, 96, 181
Coptic church, 136, 167
Counter Reformation, 99, 115, 132 ff.
Cranmer, Thomas, 108, 119 ff.
Crete, church of, 162
Cromwell, Thomas, 120
Crusades, 78, 82, 86, 91, 144; the First, 145; the Third, 145; the Fourth, 140, 146, 147
Cutler, Timothy, 201
Cyprian, 23
Cyprus, church of, 164
Cyril, bishop of Alexandria, 38
Cyril, patriarch of Alexandria, 135
Czechoslovakia, church of, 166, 167

Dakotas, 219
Danish-Halle Mission, 241
Dartmouth, 202, 208
Darwin, Charles, 220
Deacons, 15–17
Decius, 22, 23, 32
Declaration of Independence, 209
Democracy, rise of, 176 ff.
Denck, Hans, 129, 131
Denmark, 108
Descartes, René, 181
Dessau, League of, 104
Diets, German, 102, 104 f.

Diocletian, 23, 33, 35, 50, 58
Dioscurus, patriarch of Alexandria, 135
Disciples of Christ, 211, 214
Dodecanese Islands, church of, 162, 164
Dominic and the Dominicans, 88, 92, 101, 227, 228
Donation of Constantine, 76, 96
Donatists, 34 f., 52, 58
Donatus, 73
Dostoyevsky, F. M., 159
Duff, Alexander, 244
Dunkers, 206, 209, 234
Dury, John, 183
Dutch Reformed church, in the colonies, 205, 210

Economic restrictions of colonies, 203
Edessa, 137, 145
Edict of Nantes, 168, 172, 173, 179
Education, 71 ff., 90 ff., 108, 114, 116
Educational missions, 244, 245, 260
Edward VI, king of England, 120 ff.
Edwards, Jonathan, 207
Egbert, 65
Egypt, church of, 135, 136
Eliot, John, 241
Elizabeth, queen, of England, 122 ff.
Emperor worship, 2, 17, 22, 39
Empire, transfer of, 76
England, 168, 169–70, 174–79 passim, 190, 191, 194–95; Reformation in, 117 ff.
Ephesus, Council of, 38, 137
Episcopacy, principle of, 175–76
Episcopalians, High Church–Low Church controversy of,

216; as a national body, 210; and the Revolution, 209, 213. *See also* Church of England

Erasmus, Desiderius, 97 f., 103, 118

Erigena, John Scotus, 74

Estonia, church of, 166

Ethiopia (Abyssinia), church of, 136

Eugenius IV, pope, 149

Eusebius of Nicomedia, 35

"Evangelical" churches, 213

Evolution, controversy over, 220

Excommunication, 81

Expansion and entrenchment of the church, 236

Family life, Christian, 27 f.

Farel, William, 111 f.

Federal Council of the Churches of Christ in America, 224

Fénelon, François, 184

Feodor, Russian czar, 156

Feudalism, 50, 55

Finland, church of, 166, 167

Florence: Council of, 149; Union of, 149, 150, 154, 155

Foreign missions, 236

Foreign Missions Conference, 258

Forged Decretals, 76 f.

Fox, George, 184

France, 168, 169–70, 172–73, 177, 179–80, 191–92

Francis of Assisi, 87 f.

Francis de Sales, 183

Francis I, king of France, 106 f.

Franciscans, 87 f., 93 f., 127, 227, 232, 239

Frankish kingdoms, 66 f., 77

Franks, 49–50, 54, 62, 66

Frederick Barbarossa, emperor, 79, 145, 146

Frederick the Great (Prussia), 177

Frederick the Wise, 100, 102 f.

French in Canada, 231–33

French Confession, 116

French Revolution, 177, 180, 185–88

Friars, 81, 87 f.

Frontier, the, and the churches, 211–14

Fundamentalist-modernist controversy, 223–24

Galerius, 23, 33

Galicia, 153

Gallienus, 23

Gallipoli, 149

Geneva, 111 ff.

Gennadius II, patriarch of Constantinople, 150, 151

Georgia, 200, 206

German kings, 75

German Lutheran bodies, 219

German Reformed church, 205, 206, 210

German sects, 205–6

Germany, 168, 177, 178, 179, 190–95 *passim*, 198; Reformation in, 99 ff.

Gnostics, 13 ff., 29

God or Caesar, 257, 263

Gospels, 13

Goths, 49, 53, 54

Greece, church of, 162, 163, 164

Greek, study of, 74, 95 ff., 108

Gregory the Great, 57, 62, 75, 144

Grosseteste, Robert, 82

Grotius, Hugo, 182–83

Guiscard, Robert, 78

Halfway Covenant, 202

Hamilton, Patrick, 124

Harding, Stephen, 85 f.

Harvard College, 202

Henry II, king of England, 79

Henry III, emperor, 76

Henry IV, emperor, 78, 144

Henry IV, king of France, 115, 169, 172

Henry VIII, king of England, 107, 119 f.

Hepburn, 255

Heretics, 81, 88 f.

Hildebrand, Gregory VII, pope, 77 f.

Hispanic America, 226–31; Catholic church in, 227–29; Protestantism in, 230–31

Holy Roman Empire, 191

Hooker, Richard, 123, 175

Hooper, John, 121 f.

Horns of Hattin, Battle of, 145

Hubmaier, Balthasar, 128

Hugh the Great, 85

Huguenots, 168, 173

Humanism, 95 ff., 100

Humanists, 95 ff., 103

Hungary, 168

Huss, John, and the Hussites, 89, 102

Hutten, Ulrich von, 103

Iconoclastic controversy, 142

Ignatius, 19

Immigration, since the Civil War, 218

Independents, 169, 174, 175

India, 138, 243

Indian outbreaks, 218–19

Indians, Hispanic American, 227–28; Canadian, 231–32

Individualism and Protestantism, 178 f.

Industrial missions, 248

Inner light, 128, 131

Innocent III, pope, 80 f., 147; successors of, 81 ff.

Inquisition, 88, 134

Interdict, 81

International Missionary Council, 259

Investiture, 77 ff.

Iona, 61–62, 63

Ireland, Reformation in, 126, 203, 204

Irenaeus, 14

Irish Catholics, 203

Irish monks and monasteries, 83

Irish scholars, 73 f.

Isaac II, emperor, 146

Isidore, metropolitan of Moscow, 154

Italy, 177, 192, 198. *See also* Papal State

James, 10

James V, king of Scotland, 124

Jansenism, 184

Japan, 254

Japanese expansion, 252, 254, 257

Jeremiah II, patriarch of Constantinople, 155

Jerome, 46

Jerusalem, 5, 7, 8, 9, 10; conference of, 259; council of, 11; kingdom of, 145; patriarchate of, 135, 136, 137, 164

Jesuits, 123, 130, 133, 168, 170, 184, 189, 239, 247; in Canada, 231–32; in Hispanic America, 227–28

Jesus, 1, 6 ff., 10, 12, 13, 14, 15, 18, 21, 30

Jewish congregations, 220

Jews, 91

John, apostle, 9, 10

John the Baptist, 6

John Chrysostom, 41
John, king of England, 80
John III, grand prince, 155
John V, emperor, 149
John VIII, emperor, 149, 150
John X, patriarch of Constantinople, 147
Johnson, Dr. Samuel, first president of King's College, 201
Jonah, bishop, 154
Joseph, Russian patriarch, 148
Judaism, 3 ff., 11–12, 17
Julian, 39–40
Justin, 20
Justinian I, emperor, 54, 141, 142
Justification by faith, 101 f.
Juvenal, patriarch of Jerusalem, 136

Kagawa, 256
Kentucky, 214
Kiev, 152, 153
King's College, 201, 208
Knox, John, 114, 122, 124 ff., 174
Kosovo Polye, Battle of, 149

Langton, Stephen, 80
Las Casas, Bartolomé de, 228, 239
Latimer, Hugh, 121 f., 124
Latin church: of the Empire of Rumania, 147; of the Kingdom of Jerusalem, 145
Lausanne Conference, 226
Laval, François de, first Catholic bishop in Canada, 232
Laymen, religion of, 88 f.
Lefèvre, Jacques, 97, 111
Left-wing religious movements, 127 ff.
Leibnitz, 181, 183
Leo the Great, 38, 57

Leo III, emperor, 142
Leo III, pope, 69, 142
Leo IX, pope, 142, 143
Leo X, pope, 102
Leo XIII, pope, 193, 195
Lérins, island, 46–47
Liberal arts, the seven, 73
Lindisfarne, 63
Literature, rise of lay, 180 f.
Lithuania, church of, 166
Livingstone, David, 248
Locke, John, 181
"Log College," the, 204
Logos, 21
Lollards, 88 f., 124
Lombards, 54, 56, 66, 68
Long Island, 203, 205
Lord's Supper, 8, 11, 16–17
Louis the Pious, 73, 84, 90
Louis IX, king of France, 82
Loyalists, immigration of, to Canada, 209, 234
Luke, Gospel of, 13
Luther, Martin, 99 ff., 118
Lutheran church, 99 ff.
Lutherans, Colonial, 205, 206, 210; colleges of, 214; controversy among, 216
Lyons, Council of, 148

Mackay of Uganda, 249
Madras, conference in, 259
Magna Charta, 80
Makemie, Francis, father of American Presbyterianism, 204
Manzikert, Battle of, 144
Marcion, 29
Mark, Gospel of, 13
Martianus Capella, 73
Martin of Tours, 46, 62
Martyrs, 19, 21–22, 24, 41
Mary, queen of England, 114, 122, 126

Maryland, 200, 206

Mass movements, 246

Massachusetts, 201–3; Baptists in, 205

Matthew, Gospel of, 13

Medical work, 249

Melanchthon, Philip, 104, 106 ff., 112, 122, 130

Meldenius, Rupertus, 183

Meletios, patriarch of Constantinople, 163

Mennonites, 206, 209, 234

Merovingians, 67 f.

Messiah, 5, 6, 7, 10, 18

Methodism: beginnings of in America, 207, 208; frontier methods of, 211–12

Methodist colleges, 214, 221

Methodist Episcopal church: organized, 209; on the frontier, 211–12, 214

Methodist movement, 174, 185

Methodists, Canadian, 234, 235

Mexico, 229

Michael Cerularius, patriarch of Constantinople, 142, 143

Michael Romanov, Russian czar, 156

Michael VIII Palaeologus, emperor, 147, 148, 149

Middle Colonies, Baptists in, 205

Mikadoism, 252

Milton, John, 185

Minnesota, 219

Missi dominici, 71

Missionaries: in Canada, 231–32; in Hispanic America, 227–28; Society for the Propagation of the Gospel, 200

Missionary movement, 215; accomplishments of, 259; aims of, 257; motives of, 242; societies and the, 258

Missions: objections and defects, 259; organization and methods, 257

Modern missions, 242

"Modernism," 195

Mohammed II, sultan, 150, 151

Mohammedans, 247

Molanus, 183

Molinos, 184

Monastic orders (tenth and eleventh centuries), 85

Monasticism, 83 ff., 100 f.

Mongols, 153

Monophysitism, 135, 136, 137

Montana, 219

Monte Cassino, 48

Montesquieu, 180

Moravians, 206, 209, 241, 247

More, Thomas, 96, 120

Morrison, Robert, 251

Moscow, principality of, 153, 154

Münster, Anabaptists in, 128

Mussolini, 193

Mustapha Kemal Pasha (Kemal Atatürk), 163

Mystery religions, 3, 13

Mystics, 86, 131 f.

Napoleon, 188–89, 193

National states, 99 ff., 117

National Christian Council, 253, 259

Negro churches, rise of, 217–18

Nemanya, Stephen, 139

Nero, 19

Nestorian churches, 137, 138, 167

Nestorian missions, 250

Nestorius, 37–38

Nestorius, patriarch of Constantinople, 137

Netherlands, 116, 168, 169, 173–74, 178, 179

New England, Church of England in, 200–201; revival in colonial, 207

New Testament, 13; English, 118; German, 103 f.; Greek, 96 f.

Newman, Cardinal, 190

New York, 200, 206

Nicaea, Council of (325), 35 f.

Nicene Creed, 36–37

Nicholas I, pope, 75, 139, 142

Nikon, patriarch of Russia, 156, 157

Ninian, 62

Nominalism, 92, 94

Normans, 75, 78

North Carolina, 200; revival in, 207

Norway, 108

Norwegian Lutherans, 219

Novatian, 24

Nova Scotia, 232, 233

Nubia, church of, 136

Old Testament, 4, 13, 15, 21

Olga, 152

Origen, 20, 31–32

Outcastes, 244

Oxford and Edinburgh conferences, 226

Pachomius, 44, 45, 48

Paganism, 88 f., 94 f., 98

Painting, 98

Pantaenus, 31

Papacy, 56–57, 69, 75, 81

Papal State, 177, 188, 189, 191–93

Parker, Peter, 251

Patrick, 58–59

Paul, 1, 9, 10, 11, 19; letters of, 13

Paul the Deacon, 72

Paul III, pope, 133 f.

Peace of Augsburg, 171, 172

Peace of Westphalia, 172, 173, 178

Penance, 23–24, 61

Pennsylvania, 206

Persecution, of Christianity, 17 ff., 33

Persia, 137

Peter, 9, 10, 19, 56

Peter, metropolitan, 154

Peter the Great, Russian czar, 157, 158

Petrarch, 94

Pharisees, 5, 8, 9

Philadelphia, College of, 208

Philaret, Russian patriarch, 156

Philip Augustus, French king, 145

Philip of Hesse, 107

Philip I, king of France, 78

Philip II, king of France, 80 f.

Philip II, king of Spain, 122

Philo of Alexandria, 4

Philosophy: divorced from religion, 181 f.; Greco-Roman, 1, 2–3, 20–21, 26, 31

Photius, patriarch of Constantinople, 139, 142

Picts, 57, 62

Pietists, 132, 184, 240

Pachomius, 44, 45, 48

Paganism, 88 f., 94 f., 98

Painting, 98

Pantaenus, 31

Papacy, 56–57, 69, 75, 81

Papal State, 177, 188, 189, 191–93

Parker, Peter, 251

Patrick, 58–59

Paul, 1, 9, 10, 11, 19; letters of, 13

Paul the Deacon, 72

Paul III, pope, 133 f.

Peace of Augsburg, 171, 172

Peace of Westphalia, 172, 173, 178

Portuguese colonies, 228–29
Prayer-Book, English, 121, 123
Preaching, 88 f., 109
Predestinarianism, 103, 114 f.
Premillennialism, 223
Presbyterianism, 125 f., 174, 175; Colonial, 203–4; on the frontier, 211; and revivals, 213; in the Revolution, 208
Presbyterian colleges, 214
Presbyterian revivals, 207, 213
Presbyterians: as national organization, 210; Old School and New School controversy, 216
Presbyters, 15–16
Presbytery, Philadelphia, first in America, 204
Priesthood of believers, 102
"Protestant," origin of term, 106
Protestant missions, 239
Protestant scholasticism, 109
Protestantism, 99; divisions of, 170; and the state, 169, 170
Providence, Rhode Island, Baptist church in, 205
Prussia, 105
Public-school question, 215–16
Puritan immigration, 202
Puritanism, 121, 174, 175, 184–85
Puritans: Presbyterians among, 203; Separatists, 202

Quaker colonies, 201
Quakers, 169, 184, 195; in the colonies, 205, 206; Canadian, 234
Quebec, 231, 232
Queen's College, 208
"Quietism," 184

Rabanus Maurus, 74
Realism, 91 ff.
Recollet Order, 231

Reformation, 94, 99 ff.; and colonization of America, 199
Reformed church, 99 ff., 106, 116, 127
Religious education, 253
Religious life, medieval, 83 ff.
Remonstrants, 174
Renaissance, 83, 94 ff.; art of, 97 f.
Revivalism, 213–14
Revivals, Colonial, 207–8; educational influence of, 208
Revolution, the American, the churches and the, 208–9
Rhode Island, College of, 208
Ricci, 251
Richard the Lionhearted, 145, 146
Ridley, Nicholas, 121 f.
Rocky Mountain region, 218
Rome: church in, 10, 19, 20, 24, 28, 29, 34, 38, 46, 56–57; church of, 135, 140, 164
Roman Catholic church: in Canada, 231–33, 234; in Hispanic America, 228–30; wealth of, 229
Roman Catholics, 210; colleges of, 214, 215, 216; recent immigration of, 219
Rousseau, Jean, 180
Rumania, Empire of, 147, 148
Rumanian church, 165
Russia, 138, 140, 152, 153, 156, 198; church of, 154, 155, 157, 158; Great Schism in, 157; the Holy Governing Synod of, 158; patriarchate of, 155, 158; Slavophils in, 159; Soviet Russia, 159, 160, 161, 162; Westernists in, 159
Ryerson, Adolphus Egerton, 235

Sadducees, 5
Saints, cult of, 89

Saladin, 146

Saracens, 53, 54

Saul of Tarsus. *See* Paul

Sava, St., 140

Saybrook Platform, 203

Scandinavia, 190, 194

Scandinavian churches, 219

Schism, the Great, 140, 141, 142, 143; schisms between East and West, 142

Schism, papal, 82

Schmalkald, League of, 106

Scholastics and scholasticism, 92 ff., 96

Schools, monastic, and episcopal, 90

Schweitzer, Albert, 249

Science, rise of, 181–82; in nineteenth century, 190–91

Scotch-Irish immigration, 203

Scotch-Irish Presbyterians, 126 f.

Scotland, 168; Reformation in, 115, 123 ff.

Scottish Confession, 125

Scudder, John, 244

Sculpture, 98

Separation of church and state: in Canada, 235; in Hispanic America, 231; in the United States, 209

Septuagint, 4

Serampore, 244

Serbia, 139; church of, 140, 166

Serra, Father Junipero, 228

Servetus, Michael, 113, 129

Simeon, Bulgarian czar, 139

Simeon Stylites, 44

Slavery: Christianity and, 26, 28; controversy and division in churches over, 216–17

Slavonic ecclesiastical literature, 139, 152

Social gospel, rise of, 220–21

Socialism, 195

Society for the Propagation of the Gospel in Foreign Parts (S.P.G.), 200, 201, 241

Socinianism, 170

Socinians, 129 ff.

Socinus, Faustus, 130 f.

Socinus, Laelius, 129 f.

Sophia Palaeologa, 155

South America, colonization of, 226

South Carolina, 200

Spain, 169, 173, 177

Spanish colonies, 226

Spinola, 183

Spinoza, 181

Stanley, Henry M., 249

Stephen, 9

Stockholm Conference, 226

Stone, Barton W., 211

Strategic centers, 258

Suazrez, 178

Superstition, 88 f.

Sweden, 108

Swiss Confession, 111

Switzerland, 106, 109 ff., 168

Sylvester II, pope, 76

Synagogue, 4, 5, 10, 15

Syrian Christians, 243

Taoism, 252

Taylor, Jeremy, 185

Temple, in Jerusalem, 5, 8, 9

Tennent, William, 204

Tertullian, 20

Tetzel, 101

Theodore, of Tarsus, 64

Theodoric, 54

Theodosius I, 37, 40

Theodulf of Orleans, 72

Theological seminaries, rise of, 215

Theology, recent changes in, 223–24
Thirty Years' W ar, 171–72
Thomas Morosini, patriarch of Constantinople, 147
Tikhon, patriarch of Russia, 161
Timur, 149
Toleration, 115, 132
Torgau, League of, 104
Totalitarianism, 198
Trajan, 19
Trent, Council of, 134
Turkey, Republic of, 163
Turkish Empire, 150, 151, 166
Turks, 144, 145, 148; Ottoman Turks, 148, 149, 150
Tyndale, William, 118, 120

Uganda, 249
Ulfilas, 53
United Church of Canada, 235
Universities, 91 f.; in Hispanic America, 229
Urban II, pope, 144

Valerian, 22, 23, 30
Valla, Lorenzo, 96
Vandals, 49, 52, 53, 54
Vasily, Russian grand prince, 154
Verbeck, 255
Vincent de Paul, 183
Virginia, 200; revival in, 207
Visigoths, 66, 72, 84
Vivarium, 47
Vladimir, Russian grand prince, 152
Voltaire, 180

Vulgate, 46

War, churches' attitude toward, 195–98 passim
War of 1914–18: and the churches, 195, 221–22; and post-war disillusionment, 222–23
Welsh, 59, 61. See also Britons
Wesley, John, 185, 210–12
Wesleyan revival, 240
Western industrialism, 255
Westminster Confession, 202
Whitby, conference of (664), 64
White, William, bishop, 210
William the Conqueror, 78
William and Mary College, 201
William of Ockham, 93 f.
Williams, Roger, 205
Wishart, George, 124
Witchcraft, 89
Witherspoon, John, 209
Wolsey, Thomas, 119
Women's missionary societies, 245
World War. See War of 1914–18
Wyclif, John, 89, 117 f. 118, 124
Wyoming, 219

Xavier, 239, 254

Yale College, 201, 202
"Yanisari," 151

Zenanas, 245
Zurich, 110 ff.
Zwingli, Huldreich, 106, 109 f., 115, 124